Mackerel-catching, Portland, 1906 (from the Portland Museum Collection).

Published by Little Toller Books in 2022

Text © Sarah Acton 2022. With additional text by Gail McGarva,
Don Moxom, Anne Brown and Pat Corbett © the Authors 2022.
Any additional oral or transcripted voices © the Contributors 2022.

The right of Sarah Acton, her co-authors and contributors to be
identified as the authors of this work has been asserted in accordance
with Copyright, Design and Patents Act 1988.

Photos courtesy of Rod Condliffe and The Lugger Inn Collections
unless otherwise credited.

We have made every effort to trace the copyright-holders of the images;
in an inadvertent omission or error please notify Little Toller Books.

Typeset in Sabon by Little Toller Books.

Printed in Cornwall by TJ Books.

All papers used by Little Toller Books are natural, recyclable products
made from wood grown in sustainable, well-managed forests.

A catalogue record for this book is available from the British Library.

ISBN 978-1-915068-08-8

MIX
Paper from
responsible sources
FSC® C013056

Seining Along Chesil

Voices from a Dorset fishing community

Sarah Acton

with

Gail McGarva, Don Moxom,
Anne Brown and Pat Corbett

LITTLE TOLLER

(Uncle) George Randall getting the heaving line ready on top of the seine.

Contents

Seatown view (courtesy of Humphrey Bickford).

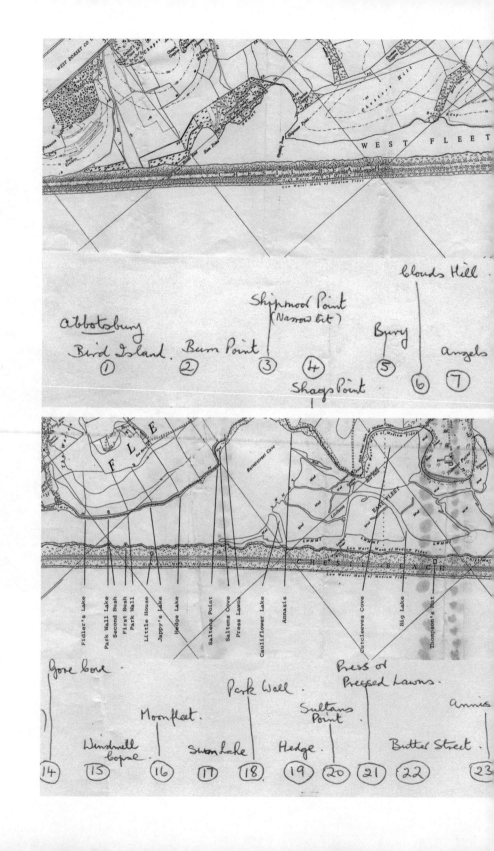

Abbotsbury

Bird Island
①

Burn Point
②

Shipmoor Point
(Narrow bit)
③

Shags Point
④

Bury
⑤

Clouds Hill
⑥

Angels
⑦

Fidler's Lake
Park Wall Lake
Second Bush
First Bush
Park Wall
Little House
Jappy's Lake
Hedge Lake
Saltens Point
Saltens Cove
Press Lawns
Cauliflower Lake
Annasis
Cutcleeves Cove
Big Lake
Thompson's Hut

Gore Cove
⑭

Windmill Copse
⑮

Moonfleet
⑯

Swan Lake
⑰

Park Wall
⑱

Hedge
⑲

Sultans Point
⑳

Press or Pressed Lawns
㉑

Butter Street
㉒

Annis
㉓

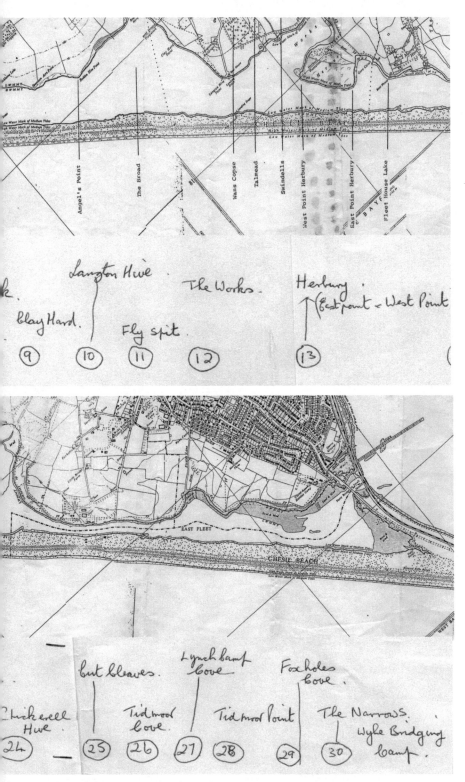

The Fleet map annotated in biro and Chickerell landmarks.

Foreword

Rod Condliffe

W e have always had family gatherings around Christmas, and every year we relate to each other the fun times and the history of when my Uncle Chum (Northover) had his fishing boats on Chesil Beach at Park Wall and, in later years, further to the west at Fiddlers Lake ('first bush'). As we have got older we have all begun to realise that the history of seining on Chesil Beach will be lost unless recorded. My cousin Celia (the daughter of Boyce Northover, Chum's brother) was researching the Northover family tree and became aware of the writer, Sarah Acton, and the book began.

My first recollection of being with my Uncle Chum was as a three-year-old; with him and his father (my grandfather), Levi Henry, collecting wood stored on the beach over the summer and taking it by trow to Press Lawns (near Butter Street) to be collected and delivered to *Ja'stan* on Gaston Hill (the family home). I remember as a nine-year-old being sent to Uncle George's cottage by Chickerell church to tell him that there was fishing at daylight in the morning, and at twilight running through a very eerie churchyard to reach his door, there to be greeted by Aunt May welcoming me into an oil-lit room full of stuffed animals staring down from the walls. I have strong memories of Sunday mornings in winter in the fields down Fleet Lane, stretching new rope to take the turns out – by tying a rope to a stout branch in the hedge – and wrapping a turn around a six-foot pole, and Charlie Legg and I pushing the pole between us down the length of the rope towards the other end where Uncle George or Uncle Chum was turning the rope through their hands.

Opposite: Inside Rab Stone's fishing store, the result of many years of beachcombing (photo by George Wright).

Scott Condliffe, Rod's eldest son, in a lerret.

In August, some seasons when the mackerel were more plentiful at the western end of the beach, Park Wall rowed a boat to Abbotsbury, and then, for transport, we either caught the 3pm bus outside the Lugger Inn, or if we were lucky, a builders merchants' lorry came along. The fishermen would clamber on piles of builders' materials in the back of the lorry and have a lift to the Ilchester Arms in Abbotsbury. From there we all walked to the beach along the footpath under Abbotsbury Castle to Ash Huddy's Hut where the boat was stationed.

One August day, when all seemed calm, Uncle Chum shouted at me as he was tending to his garden, 'Come on my son, there's some heavy seas coming, we got to go to the beach and haul up the boats.' When we got over on top of the beach the swell had already started, and by the time we had got the nets in the boat and by block and tackle pulled them to the top of Rudge, the seas were nearly over-topping the beach. How did he know something was amiss? He told me it was the sound of the sea and the seagulls, a sound he had heard once before in younger days when a similar thing had happened. Sarah relates this story again in a later chapter in this book.

When I had a motorbike, I remember riding to Moonfleet with Uncle Chum riding pillion. Unfortunately, I could never teach him how to corner – while trying to lean the bike over, he would go in the opposite direction to try to keep the bike upright. Later,

Chum Northover on the Chesil side of the Fleet working the boats in winter.

I would take him by car to Gundry's net factory in Bridport to meet up with Jack Phillips who would then take us on a tour of the works for him to choose the nets he wanted to make his seines with. When I moved away to near Start Point in Devon, I managed to get a large hauling winch which I brought up to Park Wall, and between three or four of us we managed to transport it across the Fleet and position it on top of the beach. Not long after, the double-wheel tractor came along to do some of the donkey work. The winch is still there, the rusted remainder of it anyway… all these memories and more since have been stirred up by the making of this book, the discussions and sharings.

My thanks go to Don Moxom, Gail McGarva, Anne Brown and Pat Corbett for adding their expertise and to everyone who has contributed to this shared story of seine fishing along Chesil Beach, of which Uncle Chum and the Park Wall crew make up one chapter. Sarah has managed to bring all these tales together in a way which I hope readers will enjoy.

R. C.

Freshwater Beach, Dorset

Sarah in a trow on the Fleet (photo by Dennis Harman).

Introduction

Sarah Acton

This book is interested in the cultural history and heritage of Chesil Beach, and its once-thriving seine fishing communities. By listening and gathering memories, personal stories and voices, we remember lerret boats, nets and villagers who survived by harvesting the sea by hand. The knowledge and craft, the family-lines passing tradition hand over hand, had changed very little since the fourteenth century (although it is surely much more ancient than that). Their individual and communal sense of belonging is woven into local identity by lifetimes of familiarity, family ties and experiences.

What these lifelong memories and stories might lead us to is remembering a way of life now gone – 'though at the time you take it all for granted,' as Portland fisherman and artist Rab Stone says. A fresh remembering is a longing of how to live more closely with the sea and its seasons. Perhaps this yearning gives us space to listen to the sounds of Chesil Beach, acknowledging that each one of us is a pebble rolling and rabbling a soundtrack of everyday music across its great lifespan. This book is a tribute to all those who love and have loved Chesil Beach.

Many of the fishermen I spoke to who seined as young boys and men still live within earshot or view of beach. The process of research has been organic, taking place over many months – listening, talking, reading, walking, reflecting, layering stories and personal voices arriving on a rising tide of kinetic energy. Some is spoken, some listened, some overheard. The energy is oral, live voices speaking to you. There are no facts here, only many aspects of storied truth. What you are about to read is largely undocumented in printed history, recorded by word of mouth and repetition, woven together to remember the culture and heritage of working men and women along Dorset's Chesil coastline, a rural seaboard.

S. A.
Beer, Devon

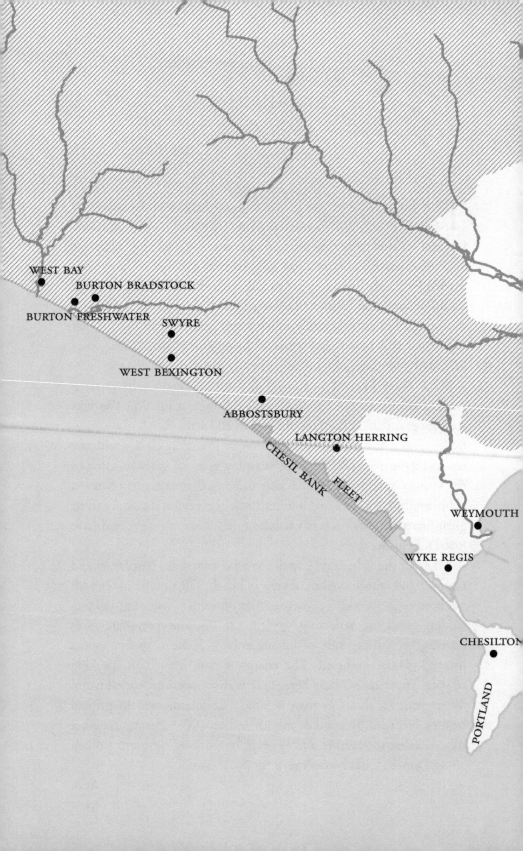

WEST BAY

BURTON BRADSTOCK

BURTON FRESHWATER

SWYRE

WEST BEXINGTON

ABBOTSBURY

LANGTON HERRING

CHESIL BANK

FLEET

WEYMOUTH

WYKE REGIS

CHESILTON

PORTLAND

The Park Wall crew launching a boat in 'reasonable seas' – Rod says they went out in most seas when others wouldn't.

A Seiner's Dictionary

Big Sea: Lyme Bay

Blen: Pout-whiting

Bunt, cod end, purse or *hose:* Bag on the end of the seine net

Heaving line: Weighted block with rope thrown ashore from the boat

Huars or *wazers*: Lookouts for approaching shoals of mackerel

Joey: Small mackerel, under-sized

Lawn or *long end:* Beach-end arm of the seine net

Little Sea: Fleet Lagoon lakes

Loat: Sections of net sewn together to form the seine

Quant: A pole used for pushing or punting a *trow* through shallow waters

Quiddle: Squid or cuttlefish

Rudd: The shadow of a large mackerel shoal

Rudge: Ridge on the sea-side of the Fleet lagoon

Ship end: Line arm of seine net thrown from boat to shore

Shot: Throwing the net from the boat to catch feeding mackerel in shallows

Slack of ebb: Brief pause at the end of the ebb tide

Stray: A ruffle of large numbers of feeding mackerel in season

Trow: Flat-bottomed boat used on the Fleet

Tutes: Dealers or fish merchants

Yark: To mend nets

Young flood: Start of the flood tide

Opposite: Seine boats at Portland and lerrets further up, with wicker pots in the foreground (postcard from Rab's collection).

I

A Way of Life

I

Everyday Life has a Music

'When you go back, you realise how important fishing was round here. If you could get a boat and the gear, you would earn a living, perhaps even a small fortune.'

Alan Arnold, Abbotsbury fisherman, still fishes with gill nets and a few years ago he made up a seine to show his son what it was like, but as he points out to me, 'It's not really about the gear, it's about the knowledge of where to go, when to fish and what to do.'

'Seine' refers to both the style of fishing and the name of the net – a drag-net for hunting pelagic mackerel, which feed in shallow waters. Seines may have been used by Stone Age fishermen. Seining is practised all along the south and south-west coast, using a Danish design of gear widely documented in the British industry from the early nineteenth century. Here in Dorset, one arm of the net ('the long end') is held ashore – traditionally by a pole or 'spek', later by men – whilst the seine net in the boat is rowed out and paid out, or 'shot', as swimming mackerel bear down into it on the tide. The boat is then circled back in a horseshoe around the fish. The net hangs in the water; lead weights pull the bottom end to the seabed and cork floats buoy the top, with a conical net bag between.

As the former Fleet Warden Don Moxom reminds me, 'Dorset seine fishing is one of the most environmentally friendly ways of sea fishing. Damage to the seabed must be minimal. The seabed slopes quickly and deeply away from a deployed net. Further out, in Lyme Bay, damage has been done by trawlers to the seabed, and one of the rare creatures put at risk out there is the coral sea fan – you saw one yourself.'

Opposite: Abbotsbury crew next to the seine boat, *Betty*, Lizzy Arnold and Ash Huddy.

My tiny sea fan, a horny coral, *Eunicella verrucosa*, was washed up ashore opposite Moonfleet Hotel. A delicate white twig, and when I picked it up Don told me how it is pale pink when alive underwater, part animal, part plant. It is now pressed into the back of my notebook, a small reminder of unexpected encounters, quietly precious.

Seining was hard physical effort. The nets were different sizes depending on the depth of the shelf off the beach, but many were big and heavy and the boat shot against the tide so that the swimming shoal were pushed into the wall of net. The men on the 'long' or 'lawn end' might be older, and often had to walk down the beach during the shot to stop the net from washing 'down tide' of the long-end arm. The whole shot was a dance. As the boat returned ashore all of the crew bar one jumped out, and younger members took the strain of the 'ship end' that was thrown or passed to them in order to haul the weight of the wet, wriggling fish. By this action, as the ship end 'heaved' and 'walked' or 'ran' towards the long end, the shoal was pushed into smaller and smaller 'loats' (net sections), arriving in the final bag of the net (variously known as the 'bunt', 'cod end', 'purse' or 'hose') before they could escape. Often boys would have to throw pebbles, herding fish, before they swam out through any gaps as the arms came together.

The work didn't stop there. Next came the effort of landing the boat on greased oars and pulling it up by the start rope, and then pulling up, winching or shovelling the fish from the net, and finally sorting, carrying and dispatching the fresh catch to the buyer. Many of the best recorded catches were landed on Sundays, when everyone in the family helped out. The sale to the fish merchant was made there and then on the beach. Mackerel caught using the alternative style of feathering, involving a line of twelve or more hooks, fetched a higher price, according to West Bay fisherman Dave Larcombe. Feathered fish are less squashed together, their stomachs are not bloated with whitebait and sprats.

Local knowledge of the tidal currents, weather patterns and seamanship skills were key to a successful catch. 'People don't realise

Abbotsbury crew pulling the net in.

'Keeping the boat.' Abbotsbury crew (with Ashley Arnold in the boat).

it was a dangerous occupation,' Rod Condliffe tells me. 'Just how much physical hard work it was. Fishermen risked their lives in a way, but there was money to be made, and they knew the ways of beach.' We are talking about hundreds and hundreds of men in dozens of small crews of twelve to fourteen over two to eight generations. Tight-knit teams of men and women who knew Chesil Beach and its moods, trusted the shore crew and captain to make split-second decisions, and as Edward Marshallsay said, 'fished as a way of life.' The work was mostly part-time, but you needed a ready and skilled crew available all summer. Although I've seen references to full-time fishermen in Portland, Wyke and other areas in the nineteenth century, there was only one full-time crew in Abbotsbury from the Second World War until the 1970s. I've heard of several fishermen reviving the seine in the 1980s, and a seine was put out inside West Bay Harbour in 2021. But for the most part the nets have rotted, been cut up or lie in storage.

Seiners follow the mackerel season from April or May to October, after which the mackerel drift deeper and further north. Over late autumn, seiners went sprat and herring fishing, fished for prawns and shrimps in winter, set crab and lobster pots and gill nets, and went eel fishing with fyke nets or 'pecking' prongs. Some of the crews also used to go wildfowling, and in the winter, beachcombing took place, as there were larger timber pieces washed off boats in the winter in those days, which were collected and taken home to use for various projects. It was always a given that any piece of wood hauled to the top of the beach was claimed and nobody else would touch it.

The lerret was a seine boat built for waves, while equally beamy square-backed boats were used for smaller seines and pots in less 'lumpy' weather. The lerret was heavy and needed plenty of hands, so a smaller crew might use the square-backed boat during the daytime before changing to the lerret with a larger net when the extra hands came on in the evenings. You might shoot the net several times if the going was good, or if it wasn't, if you didn't catch, they might say, 'That's one for the Queen.' Alan Arnold tells

Chickerell Hive crew counting out mackerel catch in spring. Among the crew are: Ted Harman and sons Dennis and Barry together with co-owners Henry 'Chappie' Beale, Les Hinton and 'Mac' Macaddan (courtesy of Dennis Harman).

me, 'Sometimes you really had to work hard for it. I remember we had ten shots once. One after the other in the *Chesil Queen* [lerret]. Twenty stone a shot so made up to two hundred stone.' Larger regular catches might be three, four hundred stone, though I've heard of bumper catches nine hundred and a thousand stone weight. But 'some years the mackerel don't come very thick. You'll be lucky if you get a hundred stone all the year and yet you have to keep working the tides to make your numbers up.'

From the early to late 1970s, many Chesil fishermen had retired, died, or given up their lerrets for the lighter square-backed wooden or fibreglass tenders suited to calmer seas. Some encouraged their families into more profitable trades, consigning seining to a weekend hobby or adventure, thereby bringing an end to a tradition, way of life and the knowledge that had spanned hundreds of summers. I get the feeling that everyone accepted the end of the heyday, like an inevitable weather pattern approaching.

Levi Henry John Northover ('Chummy' or 'Uncle Chum', 1907–85), whose memory prompted this book, was one of the last lerret seiners running a highly successful crew at Park Wall, and was of the first to retire. In 1979, he donated one of his fleet of lerrets to Exeter Maritime Museum (*Blessing*) and one to Weymouth museum (*Pleasure*) and sold one to Royston Mowlem (*Blessing Too*). Legend has it that he burned an older lerret in a Viking-style pyre. The romanticism of the fishermen reverberates through time, despite the practical and elemental hardships they faced daily.

Seine fishermen wanted better for their families. Seine fishing was hard work. It was worth it for the cash, but by the 1970s, tastes for oily fish were changing. People 'didn't want fish with a face,' Rab Stone tells me. 'If it's in a nice plastic bag, and you didn't have to do anything with it, then that was all right.' The mackerel market was weak and merchants became less willing to come down the beach. You had to have a ready buyer to sell the fish, and a good price. By this time large purse seiners were trawling off the north Atlantic and mackerel was available all year round.

But the reasons for this period of transition stretch beyond the open sea. Towards the end of the 1970s, closed coastal communities working towards communal self-sufficiency were faced with real change. Cliffs and beaches were changing shape with sea defences, holiday camps were thriving, scores of anglers had arrived, and the knowledge of how to shoot and tweak nets was a secret and dying art. The docks and harbours were changing as maritime industry dwindled, and the Chickerell brickworks closed down. The gentle rocking seasonal rhythms of summers seining mackerel and winter-life in ditches and docks was slowing, and one day it was all gone. The fish may still be around, but as Alan Arnold says, 'You can't seine unless you have a good three or more people who really know what they are doing on the beach, otherwise you can't even think about doing it.'

Chesil Beach roars and stings, silver shoals of memory dart beneath the sea surface like fragments of mirrors, as memory triggers memory. Today we balance on the sharp edge of legacy and nostalgia

Park Wall crew loading seine nets in a boat for the evening shot.

as Chesil coastal communities continue to shift, dig heels into cultural identity. Meanwhile, the longing is still here, held by those waiting for us by the driftwood fire, waiting for the heaving line to be thrown across to them, ready to help haul and heap the catch. It took many hands to manage this effort. The ancients are waiting for us to shoot our nets, throw them the rope of remembering, so that we can nourish our communities with their own heritage and story. In every voice and trembling, a bell returns.

Much is revealed in the silences, the spaces between snapshots and testimonies still crusted with salt, cigarettes, warm with sun and all of the unspoken everyday stories that will never be told. People get in touch, news spreads. I weave ladder rungs from old rope to trail behind this book. Patterns in the dialect, names and voices call across generations of mackerel, swift-skim-shimmering.

2

Chesil Beach

Run down the beach for them, shove out the boats,
scrush-scud, shoal-thrum, Away!

Another kind of listening, the old vernacular speech of beach. Cadences of fishmouths and drifting currents bring to the surface five thousand years of men and scales and shoreline. More fish than bricks. More fish than docks. More fish than fields. When the mackerel came to Chesil, they came as a body moving as one bristling shadow-sea. Little terns followed them. Gannets and gulls followed them. Men and nets followed them.

Soundtracks of pebbly backwash, shingle-crush-stone undertow of a billion individual pebbles scratching for their jumbled places along eighteen miles of Chesil Bank's high ridge, looking out of Lyme Bay over open sea towards France. Constellations of layered story rise above and dip below the tideline. Holler the crew and launch as the silver-green fish stray, 'Maaaackrel'. They nod the wink as teams fly, fly from the beach in whooshes of wooden-hulled boats rolled down greased oars and launched with a dozen hands of fisher-wisdom behind. Old men, women and small children keep the boat once the net is full, land the catch then send the boat back out to shoot the nets again. Soundtracks. Seamen, steely and gaunt, step back three centuries, step quiet along secret paths on 'darks' (moonless nights). The interior energy of these ragged smugglers whispers a web of tension that holds fast long after their landing under Hoar Head, along the ways from Moonfleet.

Chesil Beach, also known as Chesil Bank, is a curl of high-ridged shingle looking out of what was known for centuries as

Opposite: Chesil Beach ridge, looking towards Portland from Abbotsbury (photo by Sarah Acton).

Dead Man's Bay (Lyme Bay). The barrier beach absorbs the impact of endless North Atlantic waves that travel on a fetch of energy over thousands of miles, absorbs the percussion of boots, hulls, nets and oars sucking and smacking the surface of shore and sea. Soundtracks. The shoals of mackerel sing underwater melodies.

shim-shards-warm, flesh-mi-laddies-shape,
lordi-waves-us-THHHHHRRRRRRRRR

It's late autumn. I've climbed the ridge at Abbotsbury from the café to take in the long view in both directions. The isolated pebble bank is only accessible by car here, and from Wyke Regis you have to walk the high side of the Fleet. Ahead of the ridge is open water. Portland, the shoulder of the Verne citadel, rises up to the west, and in the east, the gold honeycomb of Burton Bradstock cliffs catches the sun. Below, a steep shelf of moving water splashes mouthfuls of spring tide, and each pull gouges out toothless bites or frills, known locally (in their more extreme hollows on the seaward side) as 'crubs'. The northwest wind is sharp and the sea looks defiant. I can't take my eyes off its Escher-switches over the water. There are signs warning of the fierce undertow along this stretch, and plenty of anglers.

The undertow is an arm of strength and power, pulling down harder and deeper as you go west towards Portland, depending on the tide and weather. 'None of the fishermen could swim.' I'm first told this by Celia and Tony Harrison in their Dorchester kitchen, and it is repeated in many subsequent conversations. Celia's father, Boyce, was Chum's brother, and is remembered still as outgoing, a skilled seiner and eel fisherman with one eye. Celia's family are Northovers, originally from Puncknowle, later moving to Chickerell. All of Chum's nine brothers and sisters grew up on the Fleet, out on the water with their uncles fishing and aunts picnicking on beach, everybody swimming in Little Sea over long summers in the wider pool of lagoon between Chickerell Hive and Wyke. Rod's mother, Barbara, remembers the picnics well: 'We used to take a gramophone and dance, a gramophone, can you imagine!' And they were lavish affairs judging by this account from

Park Wall crew in late 1930s.

Four-oared lerret ready to go out to sea (from the Portland Museum
Collection).

Jackie Ireland: 'The amount of food and all the stuff they used to take across for the special Sunday picnics was incredible, the trows laden down with it all; bottles of champagne, potatoes, a chip-fat fryer that Barb and Margi used to cook chips on a gas ring with, peaches, and basketfuls of good food... I'd never seen such beautiful fresh peaches.'

Jumbling the generations, I hear the soundtracks of Chesil Beach as backdrop to countless carefree childhood memories and family outings during times of relative financial hardship in ordinary working lives. It is a deep and rich personal relationship that comes across; a place to go to and from, with a lifelong territorial sense of belonging 'of' and 'to' this beach. The expanded freedoms of repeated summers and Sundays invited outdoor adventure and ease of escape for everyone who lived close by.

In a dream of salt and bream, we strain for ghosts. The golden age of documented lerret seine fishing was long before our time, in the late-nineteenth and early-twentieth century, pre-war. Black-and-white photos show a hundred or more lerrets dotted about the ridge just out from Chesilton (Chiswell), and that was just the far western end of Chesil Beach. The last of the lerret seiners – the last in a long line of Chesil fishermen – were seafarers who returned after the Second World War and revived what they knew, seining in tight family crews, their geographical territories dictated and known by the places in which they launched and landed their catches. All fishermen, like mackerel, as one shoal, know their place in time, inside the story of the seasons. And it is these men and their families that are talked about in living memory: such is the sheer force of the elements that drives linear time into a curved wave that dumps across the endless shingle days.

Last year, Rab's son, also a fisherman, found a washed-up piece of logwood on the tideline at Chiswell. Rab had seen the likes before as a young boy. The ship that had carried the logwood cargo was *The Ran*, wrecked in 1893. Logwood is distinctively heavy (a wood so dense it sinks), and its red pigment can be extracted for dye. With the help of woodworm making light (over one hundred and thirty years) and the swithering sand dunes of the seabed, the logwood resurfaced, bobbing up and out of its time. This particular item, around my height, lies in the Portland Museum at the time of writing.

Under shallow seas is a churn of fish and marine life, while a-surface there are longshore men, nets and boats. To understand seine fishing in more detail we must understand distinctions of particular physical stretches of the eighteen-mile-long Chesil Beach. There are many views as contributors remember and revisit scenes from childhood and adult life, with weather-eyes over wave-crests, shifty-eyes over shoulders, little tern-eyes, fish-eyes skywards underwater, with a warden's vigilance, a sea anemone's sensor, an oyster-catcher's chance, with seagrass and tassleweed shivers, hungry fox-eyes, beach sighs.

The word Chesil derives from the Anglo-Saxon 'ceosel' or 'cisel', meaning gravel, sand or shingle. The beach is a steep, crested ridge that carves and sculpts a raised bank of pebbles, a natural barrier that, for eight of its eighteen miles, cuts through the fields and protects the shallow tidal lagoon below, known as the Fleet. Rod Condliffe tells me about the beach as we sit around the table in his first-floor living room at Freshwater Holiday Park, overlooking the low winter sunsets of Burton Freshwater. He explains that it is often characterised and understood from its more accessible (and therefore far more photographed and documented) public-access points in Chiswell at Portland, Abbotsbury, West Bexington and Burton Bradstock.

The beach is shrinking in length with longshore drift and naturally warming climate causing sea levels to rise. Formed at the end of the last Ice Age, Chesil's lifetime spans just five thousand years, a sigh in Earth's history. There was a moment when the beach suddenly appeared, with pebbles and debris thrust up from below – tundra ledges and shelves that joined what we call England and

France. A warm thaw. This is a blink away. The pebbles remember mountains and the deserts before this. The tilt of an axis, the dust of a fossilised feeding ground.

The pebbles on Chesil are all washed eastwards in a constant process of motion, starting as sandy gravel at Abbotsbury and increasing in size to those smooth and palm-sized stones at Chiswell that you cannot pocket. Legend has it that the smugglers, while 'coastal trading', would feel the pebbles and by their size would know exactly where they had landed along the beach.

From Wyke Regis to Abbotsbury I walk wild stretches where private farmland dips down to meet the shoreline, and traditional fishing villages huddle inland at Langton Herring, Chickerell, Charlestown, Swyre, Puncknowle and Wyke Regis. Rab observes, 'There was not so much physical distance between the boats and crews on the beach, so to speak, as there was distance between the villages themselves inland. The fishermen were sited relatively close together for the seine and would see everything going on further along the beach.'

There is no Right of Way along the beach. The land adjoining the Chesil Beach is all privately owned including a few miles of National Trust beach at Burton Hive and Cogden, and the beaches owned and managed by the Royal Manor of Portland, Earl of Ilchester, and Freshwater Beach Holiday Park. The beach at Portland, though, is common land – freely accessible for 'air and (passive) recreation', and permissive access arrangements exist elsewhere. The ownership of the Fleet seabed lies with the Strangways family, the Ilchester Estates, originating from a grant to Orc (a House Carl to Canute) made by Edward the Confessor, sometime between 1041 and 1058: 'His strand all in front along his land over all, well and freely, up from the sea, and out on the sea, and all that to his strand is driven, to be his by my full command.' This appears to gift a margin of seabed on the sea side of Chesil, out on the sea, to low tide or perhaps more. The ownership by the Ilchester Estates of the Fleet seabed on the landward side runs up to the mean high-water mark.

In the Portland Local and Family History Centre there is a thin

The Park Wall crew winch a seine boat with net to the top of rudge with a tractor.

Moonfleet Manor, with the Chesil Bank and huts beyond.

folder of documents, a far soundscape away from the grunting, heaving beach. It was donated by Bob Wollage, a stonemason and poet who – alongside his friends Skylark Durston and George Davey – collected local and oral histories in dialect on Portland for the museum. It was due to their efforts in collecting and writing down old Portland ways that these are remembered, and the process of remembering continues, urgent and necessary.

There are accounts of the ridge overtopped at Chickerell in storms, and even breached. Dennis Harman, a Chickerell fisherman, whose father Ted co-owned a seine fishing business from Chickerell Hive, remembers the damage to their crew's hut on the ridge that collapsed in 1989. Somehow the wintering seine boat was thrown out of the structure rather than crushed beneath it in the force. When we went across together to look at the remains, I was struck by how substantial the concrete roof was, and shocked to see the squashed brick sandwich of hut debris below. Within the mystery of 'dynamic equilibrium' all elemental forces are consistent enough to keep the essential shape of the pyramid of pebbles despite being thrashed and battled. The wave that crushed this hut must have been immense in size and power. Were it not for this visible reminder we might be charmed into thinking the beach benign. Dennis also recalls a bolt of lightning interrupting a picnic a few years back, and another eel fisherman he knows said 'he, too, may have been struck on another occasion, he had tingles after.'

The waves along Chesil Beach have a particular pattern, and break close in to the shore. The lerret, which is a heavy clinker-built boat with bow and stern post double-ends and high gunwales, is built to surf lumpy seas and launch from the steep bank without swamping or capsizing. The fishermen knew the geomorphic shapes of the beach through a lifetime of familiarity. Edward Marshallsay tells me, 'I was on the beach helping with the catch young, stretching ropes, sorting the fish from this big, maybe three or four years old.' I later see photos of a teenage Edward with long blonde hair holding the ship arm of the seine with the older crew.

As Rod says, the fishermen knew how 'canns' formed on the

George Randall mending the seine.

The Abbotsbury crew pulling up *The Sprat* seine boat after a shot. Lizzy is spreading the arms of the seine back ready to load the boat for another shot straight away, then cover the fish in the hose to deal with afterwards.

back of the beach where sometimes in storm situations, water filters through the beach and flows under the beach causing a stream which collapses the shingle above to form these hollows. 'Uncle Chum tweaked his nets continually to account for shifting movements and occasional groundswell,' he tells me. Seining was competitive, as much for the thrill of catching as anything else, but to earn a living you had to engineer the best net, time the launch and shot, and square up to the fleeting and lightning-flash quarry. The art of the seine was an obsession with tuning and trimming the net, being alert and ready. Win or lose, it was the same effort.

Rod remembers that one afternoon when he was staying with Uncle Chum in Chickerell, something he did most summers as it was close to the beach, Uncle Chum rushed over to the Fleet to move the lerrets on the far side to safety, dragging the teenage Rod along to help. Chummy told Rod he'd only heard once, many years before, the growl of the sea breaking on the beach making a particular noise and the gulls and other birds observing this. A terrible storm was coming. It did come. In 1979, 'a high spring tide combined with a storm surge caused by disturbance far out to sea' and threw massive wave fetches to 'overtop' Chesil Beach and cause damage and havoc all along the beach. One of the last lerrets on Portland, *Christina*, was washed up over the roof of 'The Dead House' – the shed that once housed the shipwrecked and the dead. This shed still stands behind the Cove Inn at Chiswell.

In the photos of the Cove Inn beneath a giant twenty-metre wave in 2014, you can hear stories of the connecting road to the mainland being flooded, and the lower Chesil Cove roads at Brandy Row navigated by row boats – all this before the causeway and modern sea defences were finished and repaired in the mid-sixties. A storm sixty or more years before was remembered by Rod's mother, Barbara, in conversation with Gail McGarva in 2011: 'We used to stay over there with the bell tent. One night, suddenly, my father and my brother Boyce turned up and said "come home at once", as the water was lapping up around our tent.' At that time Chum would have been a young man, watching, learning from his grandfather and uncles first as a young boy at Cogden and Bexington, and later at Chickerell with (Uncle) George Randall, son of Rod's great-grandfather, John Randall.

The Randalls fished from Park Wall. John Randall had a fleet of six lerrets and George took over the family business and kept on three, one of which Barbara remembers as *Dauntless*. Lerrets are the kind of boats that last generations, if looked after well. When Chum later took over, 'that was his life, absolutely his life, he couldn't get over there fast enough,' Barbara recalls.

Standing on Chesil Beach at Chiswell with a prevailing sou' westerly moderate or fresh breeze is exhilarating, with the high energy of surface waves and their impact into the shingle ridge. The swash and backwash of each wave tumbles pebbles in its cycle. Meanwhile, the random but consistent sediment distribution of pebbles somehow sifts and thrashes out pebbles in their proper order of size along the beach bank. Vibrations hackle the neck hair in uneasy awe of such a constant deep and continuous push and shove. And this is how I understand 'dynamic equilibrium', sensed through my animal body, exciting, terrifying.

two worlds of fish and sun, a boat between
there's nothing like hunting silvery shoals
two worlds of tern and splash, mesh between

Geological notes by *Pat Corbett*

The Chesil Beach, standing 13 to 15 metres (around 45 feet) high, is one of the highest beaches in the land and the archetypal source of many pebbles. Most of the shingle on Chesil Beach started out as life in warm Cretaceous seas around 100,000,000 years ago.

Cretaceous seas were full of marine sponges and it is the siliceous spicules which make up their life-supporting 'scaffold-like skeleton' that are the primary source of much of the silica and the reason we find many sponge-shaped, or sponge-bearing, flints in the chalk or eroded out and concentrated in the shingle bank.

Originally, a blanket of chalk lay over West Dorset, East Devon and the area stretching south to where Lyme Bay is today. Underlying the chalk was a layer of greensand that hosted many silica 'flint' nodules (as you see in any chalk cliff). This blanket has been eroded, leaving masses of almost indestructible nodules, brought down by ancient rivers to be deposited in the sea, rounded initially by river transport, but strongly abraded and sorted by the sea's longshore drift and through incessant movement up and down the beach slope. Some chalk remains from this blanket can still be seen at Beer and Seaton and also inland from Chesil Beach, in the scarp above and behind Abbotsbury, for example. Occasional 'Budleigh buns', purple in colour, are additional pebbles reworked from older Triassic pebble beds to the west on the Devon coast.

This resistant material was initially deposited in rivermouth bars (like those we see today at locations such as Budleigh Salterton, Sidmouth and Branscombe) and some way south and west of the present location of Chesil Beach. Waves with up to eight thousand kilometres' reach (ie, from across the Atlantic) swept these up as sea levels rose after the last Ice Age. The softer underlying Jurassic clays were eroded to form a convenient bedrock ramp against which the pebbles and cobbles were rolled against each other and swept up to form a protective bank and lagoon which has eventually slowed the erosion. The low Jurassic oyster-shell-bearing cliffs

Seine boats under Golden Cap (courtesy of Humphrey Bickford).

of Langton Herring would provide little resistance to the influx of the scavenging sea, were it not for this effectively armoured, natural barrier. Storms occasionally top the beach – and rising sea levels mean that more overtopping might be likely to occur in the future. The amount of material trapped by Portland Bill (and the weathered-out black cherts of the Portland Stone are also responsible for some of the resistant material at the southern end of Chesil Beach) will hopefully be enough to hold the sea back.

Chesil Beach, a storm-driven barrier beach, formed during rising sea levels, is commonly described as shingle beach, but 'shingle' isn't a geological term. It's a term with many uses – in medicine, metallurgy, architecture – but not in geology. Geologists would use the following terms: sand (up to 2 mm), granule (up to 4 mm), pebble (up to 64 mm), cobble (up to 256 mm) and above that – boulders. So from Bridport to Portland we go progressively from granule to cobble – sorted by the natural mechanism of longshore drift. Pebble is about where it gets sore on bare feet – which is in fact along most of Chesil Beach.

3

The Fleet

In autumn, the oak leaves linger, fall at last and lie along the wooded stretches of Fleet Road to Moonfleet, and I park at Holy Trinity Church, a damp secret place with a sparse graveyard. When Celia and Tony Harrison married here in 1974 they had to get permission from the bishop of Salisbury. It was the first marriage at the church since the War thirty years before. Fleet village is scattered, depleted since its glory days as a thriving waterside manor and port controlled by the King, as recorded in the Domesday Book, and later gifted to The Priory of Christchurch at Twynham, but that was a long time ago. The current village church is a second and later replacement for the old twelfth-century church which was, famously, partially destroyed in the great storm of 1824. All that remains is the small chancel, inside which a marker shows where the storm waters reached nine metres. This old church is something else, a threshold we pass to access the Fleet lagoon along ancestral flight paths of migrating smugglers, eager seiners and scavengers of cargoes washed up on shore. The tomb below the church was once the store for contraband barrels, perhaps.

The Fleet is a natural lagoon with mudflats exposed between tides. The Fleet runs eight miles long from Wyke Regis through Little Sea and the Narrows to the main lakes and along to its terminus in brackish backwaters where an ever-changing mix of salt waters meets fresh towards Abbotsbury. From afar, a giant's footprint. Up close, the Fleet is a map of individual lakes and fields, access and launch spots and breeding grounds for terns and swans, and, below the surface, mullet and eels. A vector of worlds. A feudal throwback to wealthy lawful rights over salt, fish and eels for the

Opposite: Park Wall crew left to right: Chummy Northover, Stan Northover, Wally Randall, Meg Northover, Barbara Condliffe (née Northover).

benefit and enjoyment of the Abbot and lord of the manor. There is a swanherd at Abbotsbury Swannery whose post dates back to the reign of Henry VIII, though swans were kept by earlier Benedictine monks before that as a delicacy.

In more recent memory, swanherds Fred Lexster, John Fair, Dick Dalley and Dave Wheeler have overseen Abbotsbury's unique colony of swans. This entails not only the critical management of breeding pairs, their eggs and newly hatched cygnets on the communal nest site, but also protection for adults and fledged young at their winter feeding grounds in the mid-Fleet opposite Langton Herring, Fleet, Chickerell and Little Sea. The seabed of these shallow waters is clothed in the swans' preferred food – sea-grasses (aquatic flowering plants) – and they are joined by other swans from local rivers and wetlands.

Since the 1980s, up to a thousand birds have been herded up the Fleet every two years to be marked and undergo a health check. These 'round-ups' can only take place in July when the swans are moulting and therefore flightless, and provide important scientific data which is used for the benefit of swans internationally. The round-ups are quite a sight, with many helpers needed to herd the swans from the mid-Fleet to a prepared site at the Swannery. Flags are waved in trows to push the swans forwards, whilst teams wade into the Fleet from the land shore to join the flotilla of boats... where, eventually, the birds are encircled and gently ushered onto the shore into holding pens.

The story goes that Uncle George Randall came out of the Navy with a medal and a pay-out, and he, Chum and Boyce walked one Sunday morning from Chickerell to Abbotsbury to look at a lerret. This is around a seven-mile walk each way on the beach and inland through fields at Rodden Hive and West Abbotsbury. They knocked on the door of the cottage they'd been sent to only to find that the fisherman was out rabbiting. So they walked to Ashley Chase and found him and struck a deal. They paid £75 for the lerret and walked back the following Sunday to row it back to Park Wall. The Park Wall crew was run by Uncle George and Chum. By

Moonfleet Hotel.

The Pier at Chickerell Hive when it was intact. Now a ruin, only a couple of cross-planks remain (courtesy of Dennis Harman).

George Northover mending nets.

The Park Wall crew landing a catch, gauged from the photo as 150 stone of fish.

the 1960s, the crew, known as 'the Park Wall Officers', had moved across from where they used to load loose fish in the trows at Press Lawns to Fiddler's Lake, nearer Fleet Manor, so that fish merchants such as Cutty Thorner and, later, Gaffer Bartlett, could pull up on the hard and load the fish. Rod's Uncle Jack (Chum's brother) often drove Bartlett's truck all the way to Billingsgate market overnight. Rod remembers as a boy that the trows were laden with loose fish up to the seats (in the days before Greenslades provided cardboard boxes) and quanted to Press Lawns.

Park Wall is the trace of a wall, the print and shadow of a structure jutting out from the Fleet bank. Pointing to the west, Rod shows me 'first bush' and 'second bush', two landmarks of planted tamarisk bushes on the ridge, or 'rudge', as it's known locally, still sheltering a shed and gear. We stand on the foreshore and I hear the pumping pedals of the eager Park Wall crew, cycling along a narrow path behind what is now a low fence. We look at the mooring posts at Fiddler's Lake further round the corner where trows were once ready to punt at speed across the water to launch the lerrets. The foreshore is strewn with dry, black eelgrass, like ash. Rod says that, 'when a trow was filled with rainwater, it was tipped on its side to get most of the water out, but to dry the boat completely, dry eelgrass was used to mop up the residue, especially before putting loose mackerel in the bottom of the trow for transport across the Fleet in the days before they were boxed.'

There is an eerie bleakness to the Fleet in mid-December. A winter loneliness. Once, a century or two back, the whole coastline was remote and lonely, a dangerous place where only working fishermen ventured. Today, I find calm once I get to the Fleet's landward shore from the road, walking down from the church to the path by Butter Street, looking only ahead to the glistening waters that glimmer in double-vision, with the ridge slitting the horizon, and a crowd of pebbles chattering both near and far all at once. The walk from Chickerell for the fishermen would have been nearer a mile, but this was the usual route for Park Wall, the Chickerell Hive crew walking or cycling another lane accessed behind the Wyke Regis training camp, past the coastguard cottages.

Fleet village is the home of Moonfleet Manor, once the house of the Mohuns, and now a grand hotel. There are smuggling connections, possibly a secret passage, definitely ancient tombs at the original storm-battered church, where the trickster ghosts of Elzevir, John Trenchard and so many other coastal tenants and non-landowners, dead and alive, toil in and out of risk and adventure at the sharp end of survival in a remote spot where marginal communities exist as frontiersmen and outliers. John Meade Falkner was a young lad when his father, a curate scholar called Thomas Alexander Falkner, moved to Weymouth in 1871. By this time the great storm of 1824 had washed away part of Fleet's Butter Street and the old church, already a curiosity and resonant with echoes.

Since the beginning of the twentieth century, there has been a significant military presence on the Fleet and Chesil. Royal Engineer units from all over the country have exercised on the Fleet in the Narrows and received weapons training on the range at Tidmoor. A gunnery and rocket target range was proposed opposite the West Fleet in 1930s, but following a successful petition to the Houses of Parliament led by Lord Ilchester, the range area was adjusted. The Fleet is famously remembered as being one of the sites used for the development of the Second World War's bouncing bomb. After the war, Rod Condliffe's grandfather was sent by the local fishermen to represent them in a campaign to keep the beaches open so that they would not lose their livelihoods. It was a successful campaign and the firing range area was restricted to the limits still currently in place, protecting fishing at Moonfleet and Langton Herring. A flag goes up when they are firing.

Apart from the wall of the butts and a path leading to it, nothing remains of the firing range established on the beach at Portland. The anti-tank blocks or 'Dragons Teeth' on the inner flank of Abbotsbury Beach can still be seen, but little is left of Chesil's many wartime buildings, piers, pill-boxes and gun emplacements.

One of the last reminders are the remains of two wooden piers that stood opposite each other and were used by the Chickerell Hive crew for loading boxes of fish. Small stumps of posts remain, and I note the sunset photo of the Fleet-side pier disappearing into pastel shades of water and sky on Dennis's kitchen wall, which adds to a sense of a lost arcadia, just out of reach.

Many of the Chickerell fishermen worked at the Chickerell Brickworks or Weymouth docks. Rod tells me that Uncle Chum was reprimanded twice for not doing overtime at the docks, but the fish were on, so he joined his men to cycle and run down Fleet lane and Butter Street to reach the punted shallow-water trows at Park Wall, racing not to miss the lift over the back water to the rudge. More hands would be needed to secure the catch, unload, turn about and shoot the seine again. You needed ten to fourteen in a team. Only five went out in the boats – four oars and someone to shoot the seine, someone with experience. Dennis tells me, 'We'd get up at four in the morning early us younger ones – myself, Terry Hinton, my brother Barry and brother-in-law Stuart Bell, go across and fish, then you see there'd be older crew, retired, see, and you'd leave them to sort and pack the fish and go off to work, then we'd go back again after work to shoot the nets in the evenings.'

For the Chickerell Hive, Park Wall and Langton Herring teams, there was the added physical complication of crossing the Fleet to get to and from the rudge. Crews at Chesil Cove, Abbotsbury and Burton Bradstock could walk or sled baskets and boxes across the beach and load straight into lorries, although even at West Bay, from the square-backed tenders, Richard Larcombe says the going was hard, 'two steps forward, one back'. For the Fleet crews, the extra obstacle of packing boxes on the far side, quanting in trows across the water and carrying the wet fish in two-stone baskets, then later cardboard boxes, to the lorries did not stop them from landing huge catches, all shoulders equally ripe and raw with fish slime, scales and sweat.

A young lad of seventeen, Clive Mowlam, drowned crossing the Fleet in April 1972 on the way back after fishing when his trow, stacked full of cardboard mackerel boxes, capsized. Many watched from the far shore including his younger brother, but

Park Wall crew hauling arms of the seine.

Speading the nets on top of beach at Park Wall.

they couldn't do anything about it. Les Hinton was on board and survived, though the waters were deep, but Clive didn't come back up and it took more than half an hour to find him. Neither could swim. Sandra tells me that her father, Henry 'Chappie' Beale, and the whole community were absolutely devastated. 'It was hard for them to go on after that.' There is not so much water in the Fleet today, and Dennis remembers the Chickerell crew maintaining the channel by dredging it with a huge tractor tyre dragged by a boat.

When I think of the chance elements, the gambles, I think of smugglers walking the same paths with weight on their backs. In the early golden days of 'free-trading' (smuggling) from the mid-eighteenth century to the early-nineteenth century, an unskilled labourer might earn half a crown or five shillings for a successful night's load. In the same era a farm labourer might typically earn one to three shillings a week. Worse, this might be part-paid in corn below the market price (bear in mind that with the quarterly payment system you would be in debt to a farmer overlord as you ran up costs including rent arrears before quarterly earnings).

Dennis tells me it wasn't about the money, it was about 'the camaraderie of doing something we loved, and there was never a disappointment if we didn't catch.' Even so, they did catch often in a good season, and the money was good.

In more recent times, after shooting the nets and landing bumper catches, Edward Marshallsay, one of the younger Park Wall crew fishermen, tells me that crewmen were full of adrenalin, and would race bicycles home along the path after a night of rowing and heaving vast stone weights of fish up and over the bank before winch or tractor. Tony Beale the policeman, who was sometimes on 'the tea-time crew', always won the race even with his heavy policeman's bike. Edward lived for fishing. His eyes shine as he recounts these days: 'We lived for it, it was all we could think of.'

Fleet Field Notes by *Don Moxom*

Chesil and Fleet Nature Reserve is heavily protected by a range of national, European and global designations. These are, respectively, as follows: Site of Special Scientific Interest (SSSI), Grade 1, notified in 1986; Special Area of Conservation (SAC) designated in 2005, and Special Protected Area (SPA), classified in 1985; RAMSAR site, 1985. All of the Reserve is included in the East Devon and Dorset World Heritage Site (2001). Specific to human activity, rules have been set and guidance given by Natural England and its predecessors, the Environment Agency and its predecessors, and local authorities. Fishing activity is governed by the Southern Inshore Fisheries and Conservation Authority (SIFCA). Wardening is mainly funded by the Ilchester Estates. The wardens work to a management plan drawn up by conservation organisations, local and national authorities, and representatives of local interests.

The territory of the Fleet and Chesil and their resources involved complicated negotiations, and a dance of ancient understandings, marriages, licences and tolerances between seine crews and particularly between local families and the landowners. What was happening before the Fleet's first recorded landowner, Orc, arrived in the eleventh century will probably never be known, and possibly some of the issues that have dogged landowner and local families over the centuries since may have been inherited from far-distant periods of time.

As far back as the fourteenth century, the Abbot's control over fishing, though established, was challenged by local fishermen. In 1398, John Sparkeford was charged in the manor court for selling fish he had caught without paying the Abbot his tithe, or tenth, of the catch. In 1400, two men of the East Tithing (Elworth and Rodden), Robert Carnam and Walter Brodie, were fined 2*d.* each for keeping in their possession 'the Lord's prise of 400 mackerel out of the 4,000 they had caught,' and selling them.

Don Moxom in a trow on the Fleet (photo by Sarah Acton).

Another controversy was raised the same year by fishermen of neighbouring Langton who claimed the Abbot had prevented fishing in the Fleet and on the High Sea 'within the jurisdiction of the Admiralty'. This raised at least two problems: the extent of the Abbot's rights within the Fleet, and beyond the Chesil Beach. This time two inquisitions were held before different jurors: both declared that the Fleet had never been in the jurisdiction of the Admiralty, but the soil and water there belonged to the Abbot, and that the Abbot had not stopped anyone fishing on the high sea. The Abbot was found 'not guilty', and this seems to have put an end to the concerted campaign against him by the fishermen, who had used one argument after another against his rule.

There were more infringements brought up before the manor court. In 1439, Thomas Newman, John Poreys and others were charged in the court of frankpledge for taking eels in the West Fleet without licence after Easter, and in 1501, Benedict Weaver of Elworth and William Abelmanne were 'common fishers' (unlicensed) in 'les Fletes' and were fined 20d. each. That the Fleet was recognised as having several parts at this period is significant for later challenges. When the Abbot leased East Bexington to John Jacob in 1487, he excluded the prize of fish from the lease, retaining that for his abbey.

When Henry VIII sold the site and manor of the abbey to Giles Strangways in 1543, the deed specifically included 'all the fishery of the water called the Fleet'. The fishermen may have hoped that now the Abbot had gone they might be able to change matters to their advantage.

Apparently some tried to make new rules. The former Abbot, Roger Hardy, who was by this time Vicar of Abbotsbury, wrote to Giles Strangways, explaining some details of the fishing customs and rights he had inherited, because he thought the fishermen were trying to take advantage of their new overlord.

By the nineteenth century, fishing on the Fleet was sometimes in conflict with game preservation and the Swannery. In 1800, Thomas Earl of Ilchester gave directions for the destruction of all trows and boats found in the East and West Fleets after 12 May 1800, and his gamekeeper was instructed to seize any 'Fishing Nets, Angles [small fishing hooks], Leaps, Pipes, Baskets, Lines, Hooks or other Instruments for taking fish.' Gamekeeper John Hunt found Langton men spearing eels off Abbotsbury but whenever the gamekeepers appeared the men rowed out of reach or left their boats and ran off. The keepers did destroy three boats, and another in 1807 from Elworth. Eel fishing was a repeated trespass. John Swaffield reported eleven boats spearing on 16 January 1860, thirty-five the day after, and thirty on 19 January, but the men took no notice when ordered to stop. He could supply five names of people he had recognised from Langton and Chickerell. At least three Chickerell men were imprisoned and the Chickerell curate wrote to Lord Ilchester expressing the men's remorse and pleading for their release. Lord Ilchester replied that they had been warned several times. He said he had prepared a court case against men from these villages to protect Abbotsbury fishermen from competition, his swans and ducks from disturbance, and to preserve his royalties.

From the beginning of the twentieth century and certainly after the Second World War, as the mackerel fishery strove to re-establish itself, the relationship between the Estate and seine fishermen had changed. As far as it is known, no rents or tithes were taken and possibly had not been for decades before this. The Estate facilitated the Langton crew accessing the beach 'beyond the Abbotsbury Parish boundary' when a catch required it, and generally did not interfere with this activity. But then, in the 1970s, tensions between the two – though to a much lesser degree – were revived. Birds were the issue but not swans, and nature conservation was at the heart of the matter rather than commercial interest.

Two national surveys conducted in 1967 and 1971 detected a serious decline in the numbers of breeding terns, including the populations on Chesil. Human disturbance was considered the main problem. Dorset County Council set up a working party which included the landowner, the local authority and nature conservation representatives to seek a way of halting the decline. Recommendations included setting up a wardening scheme and one of the specific recommendations was to investigate ways of controlling the wide-tracked and noisy tractors used by the seine-netting crews and divers, vehicles that were viewed as a serious threat to the terns.

The wardening scheme was started in 1974. A trow was moored at Chickerell Hive Point, the best location for watching over the major concentrations of birds on the beach opposite. At the beginning of every nesting season, the colonies were roped off with signs asking the public to avoid the nesting areas. With the help of volunteers, the birds' nesting progress was monitored almost daily, usually from the trow temporarily moored in mid-Fleet. Even in

Boyce Northover kneeling outside the hut on top of beach with friends.

this remote part of the beach an increase in human activity was taking place. Chesil was being used as a pedestrian thoroughfare between Abbotsbury and Portland for hikers, sponsored walkers, Army units undergoing physical training and even school groups. Recreational anglers living in the county and beyond were accessing the land shore and crossing the Fleet in fibreglass dinghies. People staying in nearby caravan sites were exploring the Fleet and Chesil in inflatable craft. Dogs taken onto the beach by locals and visitors were not controlled. Schoolboys came to take eggs for their collections, but worse than that were the adults who illegally stole the eggs of these rare seabirds (there is only one other colony of little terns in the South West and Wales) to sell to collectors.

But as we were to see, it hardly mattered in the end. It has been placed on record that within a few seasons, predation – particularly by foxes – was found to be the chief cause of the birds' demise on the beach. Lack of food, predominantly whitebait, was sometimes cited as a factor contributing to both the terns and the fishermen forsaking the beach more or less together. The common terns are now restricted to an artificial island in the Fleet, whilst the little terns only survive with difficulty behind a wall of electric fencing on the beach at Ferry Bridge, where they are watched by wardens on a twenty-four-hour basis.

To their credit, the Chickerell crews, accustomed as they were to having the beach to themselves, soon accepted the situation in which all human activity including theirs was being scrutinised. They could see how this natural coastline was being disturbed. Ironically, it was an environment of which they were champions in their own way. If for any reason they had to access the colonies, they would note the nests, and marked them with sticks to avoid treading on the eggs and chicks. They policed visiting egg-collectors and shooed them off. The terns were their 'mackerel-birds', birds that came and went with the mackerel season. They warned the fishermen of the coming of the shoals as they glided out from the beach and dipped in the sea for whitebait, the prey of both bird and fish. They even had names for the two species of terns that were breeding here. The 'mackerel birds', specifically common terns, were also known as 'sternies'; the little terns were 'potters' – an apt nickname for these small birds that more commonly hunted the Fleet.

Within a few seasons, a rapport was established between the fishermen and the wardens, who sometimes lent a hand (unpaid of course) with the nets. There were some big men with burly forearms in the crew: Les Hinton, Gordon 'Mac' McCadden, Ted Harman and 'Chappie' Beale, whilst others like Sid Peach and Bernie Farrell were of a slighter build. Even going to and leaving their nets they moved in harmony, whether it was forming a procession of trows crossing the Fleet or walking in column up the beach on a path of driftwood. Most wore flat hats and worn, woolly sweaters. All had flannel trousers stained with salt water and leather boots drenched a thousand times. All are fondly remembered for their yarns and advice freely given in quiet moments on the beach in between shots or while waiting for the crew to assemble on the Fleet shore.

I am not sure, but I may well have eaten some of the fish caught by Chummy Northover and his crew in the fifties. I was a lad then living in Victoria Park, Dorchester. Every spring, my mother, along

Picnics on the beach with a bell tent (courtesy of Rex Ireland).

with many others in the road, waited for an old van to arrive with a couple of men inside it, and one of them to holler out 'Fresh Weymouth mackerel, fresh Weymouth mackerel!' Of course, the fish were caught off Chesil but not everyone had heard of that bank of pebbles. Anyhow, what a picture it was, all these housewives, knotted headscarves and aprons, money and plates ready, queuing up for the fish for tea.

Talking of hearing the beach, there were a few occasions every year when you could actually hear it a long way away. Mighty storms way out in the English Channel would sometimes produce swell waves that would travel for miles, reaching the shore in perfectly still conditions but with sufficient force to push the shingle up the beach. After every wave the grating noise of the pebbles being dragged back down in the returning water would be carried on a gentle breeze over Hardy's Monument which in those traffic-free, pre-Poundbury village days was quite audible to those living on the west side of Dorchester.

Whenever we could, my wife Liz or I would pick up our son Edgar, and his chum, Chrissie Homer, from the school bus at Langton Herring and take them down the rough track to the Fleet.

Jack Northover, Chum and George Randall with their lerret and G.R initialled baskets.

There at break-neck speed these youngsters would quant a trow across the lagoon and race up Chesil Beach to join the crew fishing in the lerret, *Vera*. The boys didn't see it quite like that at the time but they had joined an outdoor classroom in the school of working life. Captain Ernie Ayles and his stalwarts – Ian Reeder, Richard Andrews, Bob Payne, 'Cush' Denman and Roy Groves – were pleased to see the lads with legs substantially younger than theirs just as much as the boys were pleased to be there but they were careful not to show it. Gentle though the commands of the seniors were, if they went unheeded the lads would be on the end of a string of scalding remarks. They soon learned what to do. Though now the fellowship has gone, the value of it remains with them, as does the love of beach and fishing.

4
Mackerel

'It's no fish ye're buying. Its men's lives.'
Sir Walter Scott

It's the end of October and I'm standing on the shoreline in Beer about to allow gravity to overtake me on the steep incline for an early-morning dip. It is a bright, beautiful stirring, with the fishermen preparing to take out fishing daytrippers before the end of another season, and the sea is flat or 'dab-like', as they say. One of the boats, *Sambe*, hovers a few yards out, a fisherman, strains over the side, pointing. Suddenly around my legs the whole water is dark and alive. A startling, jumping-mouthed bristle of intense movement, and a thickness as the watery, lithe body flexes muscle as if in murmuration. Sprats. Dave Larcombe mentions sprats off West Bay weeks later. 'Yes, we fished them,' he says. Tiny flashes. Fleshy eyes.

Begin in the wet dark under. Begin. Splash in an ocean. Mackerel eggs are spawned in schools of millions, drifting miles in the floating silence of the upper surface layers of underwater North Sea waters. When the eggs finally hatch against all odds of tide, current and predator, the young mackerel feed in deep waters and rise to surface waters at night, but for most of their lives they are surface-living fish in summer seas. They migrate to deeper northern winter seas. Fast-forward two to eight summers, and the entire purpose of this silver fish with green-blue sheen is to follow food. The shoal flexes as one unit, the individual involuntary. The swarming school dashes, banks and twirls in a tense vibration and switch. There is no dreaming rest for a mackerel, only season and tide.

During summer migration from May to October, mackerel feed in shallow waters along Chesil among favourite ancient haunts,

Opposite: George Randall *yarking* (mending fish nets).

The Park Wall crew cutting and 'dipping out' the full seine net hose.

following sprats and whitebait caught in the shallows, forced landwards by their pursuers. As the mackerel feed, they form a dark shadow disturbing the surface... this is 'the rudd', or as Pete Stevens and the Abbotsbury crew say, 'a trip of mackerel'. Fishermen keep lookout and wave when the mackerel are straying. Otherwise they try their luck and take a shot on instinct. The straying shoals are large but 'harder to catch, they move so quick, sometimes we preferred to just take a lucky shot,' Dennis says. His father Ted Harman, a carpenter, was part-owner of two seine boats (one lerret, one flat-backed) and two seine nets at Chickerell Hive as part of a syndicate, and had a good eye for the fish. He'd say, 'Look at that rudd there, just look at it,' excited as the shadow loomed.

The seine nets were the key. 'You had to fish right and the old man was forever making adjustments,' says Dennis. 'They'd get the nets made up and then tweak them and if they weren't catching for a while they'd get Dicker, one of the older fishermen, to take a look and he'd get them to put a man at each end and see how it hung and say something about it.' At Park Wall, Uncle Chum was

West Bay fishermen, among them Ash Huddy, hauling in 12–1,400 stone of sprats and getting very wet putting the slings on while the terns dive in. Joe Laver, in the water, tries to stop fish from rolling over. The men would have dipped out the sprats on landing, a job taking two to three hours.

an expert, he would spend 'hours, days tweaking and constantly making adjustments ... all winter with the nets strung up in the greenhouse at the back of *Ja'stan* [his house],' Rod recalls.

If you were reading the London papers in June 1880, you might have read this headline, 'Food for the Gulls', referring to catches so large in Abbotsbury that the fish could not be taken onwards to markets via Upwey railway or other carrier in the heat and hundreds of tonnes were left to rot on the beach. There are plenty of similar stories throughout the hottest summers over the early-twentieth century. Where the catches were too big they flooded the market, rotted out, no good even for fertiliser on the farms. When mackerel were important to the British diet, Dorset catches were regularly reported in London papers. The fish were like silver and the other metals listed as important commodities to be taken note of; they mattered.

During in-conversation events we hear that two-stone or, for Abbotsbury, four-and-a-half-stone baskets of wet, slimy mackerel were carried on fishermen's backs to be packed in crates, then by the 1970s they were packed in cardboard boxes supplied by the fish merchant and by this time met by a refrigerated lorry. 'In the earlier days there was no ice or refrigeration lorry.' The fish died quickly on the beach – 'they don't last long out of the water,' David Larcombe tells me, then they were hawked on the beach to holidaymakers, or sold to fish merchants who had been called from a public telephone box, or they would just know to turn up expecting the catches. The buyer's lorry came down to meet the crew as they carried the baskets up from the shoreline and the journey to market was a dash to get the fish sold at Crewkerne, Poole or Billingsgate markets, and onto plates. Many Abbotsbury and Burton crews also sold fish out of the back of small vans in local villages and, as Don remembers, on Dorchester streets. Samways of West Bay started a business selling catches from a crate on the harbour wall. If there was a tiny catch, crews might cook up mackerel in a bucket and eat them on the beach.

In June 1869, the *Bridport News* reported a thresher shark caught in amongst two thousand mackerel by Wyke fishermen George and Joseph Stone. Dennis and Pete also mention seeing these, as well as basking sharks. As Rab explained to me, when a shark gets caught in the net, not so unusual, you can either roll back the net and lose the whole catch to free the shark, or bring it ashore with ropes and slings or hooks. He also tells me that when his crew did this with a basking shark and tried to use the cut-up shark meat for bait, they caught nothing with it. A Dorset story made the national papers in 1938 when Fred Farn of Chickerell wrestled a 'moby dick' shark out of his net and killed it with a penknife. Nets also caught the odd jellyfish 'blubbers', monkfish, quiddles (squid) and skate...

There are records of 'the beckons' before 1880, and this is mentioned to me as a practice right up until the end of the seine industry. A coat or pot (a 'Guernsey jumper' in Langton) was hoisted on the blade end of an oar to signify a catch, to send for help to haul it in and get in the shot if there weren't enough crew to hand. 'But someone was always on watch, always' through the whole fishing season. Rab Stone says: 'You'd put the beckon up if the fish turned up and you didn't have enough men to take a shot. They used to make me do it. You take an oar out of the boat and if you're ten or eleven years old it's quite a thing. You put a fish pot on top at the blade end of the oar; you walk it up and it'd be twelve foot high. You'd put the beckon up to get men over to help launch the boat. You had to stand there holding it up. Wherever the fish were the beckon went up. Seeing the beckon, help would soon come to get in the shot, money.'

Alan Arnold tells me about another signal, at Abbotsbury: 'Back in the older times, if you were seen to be fraternising with other crews on the beach, they'd stand an oar upside down on the beach so as to say, you're over there now, you can stay there with that crew, you've done it now.'

On the rudge it is very exposed. 'Bowers', crude canvas shelters, were built as wind-breakers for fishermen to huddle under whilst waiting for the mackerel, drinking tea and playing card games such as Euchre. Later the Park Wall youngsters built a hut, and when the Estate's man came to knock on Chummy's door, he said he didn't have anything to do with it – only the Estate wondered if he would like the right to build a temporary seasonal hut for a shilling a year, to be taken down each winter? He did. Pete Stevens tells me when I ask about lerrets that the old ones were sometimes 'cut in half to make a shelter for the crew to sit in'.

Ash Huddy had a wooden hut with a telephone line later installed to call the buyers. There was room for everyone inside. Alan remembers the between times when 'they used to be sat in that hut and they'd tell stories over and over again and you'd be sat there thinking, I've heard this one a thousand times but you daren't say anything as a young'un. "Somebody found some gold over there..." this and that story... all sorts they told, repeated over and again. That's how they used to remember together. Here we go again we'd be thinking.' When Ash's crew travelled on his Bedford truck to fish west at Portland or Chickerell they seemed to outsiders as

A 'bower' shelter on the beach (courtesy of Rex Ireland).

Mackerel catch in the hose of the seine net, pulled by winch and tractor and pushed up by (left to right) Ted Harman, Terry Hinton, Dennis and Barry Harman (courtesy of Dennis Harman).

'tough and quiet'. A tight crew, they knew each other well through long working weeks and months and years.

I get a glimpse of the resting times at Chickerell from Dennis: 'When there was someone new, a visitor or such, the old boys would tell stories about certain times when it'd been rough and they'd taken a chance. There was Sid Peach, he would tell the stories.' This was a time when older men would sit out together all day rather than home alone, and on Portland it was the same: 'It was the company and fresh air, but mainly the company that kept them going,' as Rab recounts. 'Sometimes we had really old men down on the beach into their eighties.' If they stayed out all day, the retired crew would cook up fresh mackerel in salt water. Pete tells me that the Abbotsbury crew were friendly and the kettle was always on. 'We worked really hard, people just don't realise how tiring the work was. Sometimes we'd be at beach at four in the morning and get home at ten at night, we'd sleep on the beach or in the hut between shots. We'd always have a cooked breakfast, bacon and everything.'

Soundtracks. Polyphony. Contrasts. Fast and slow. Loud and soft. Plain song. Time in its silent universe pierced with star-prick fish-eyes rolling over in underwater sunlight.

By the time the younger crew members were taking the fishing 'more seriously' in their late teens or early twenties, and if 'we'd behaved,' they were on a full share of the seine. Edward Marshallsay says he was on 'quarter share aged around ten or eleven,' and Pete tells me that at Abbotsbury, 'if you could carry a pot of fish up the beach and if you could row, you'd have a full share by thirteen or fourteen, if you got on the boat that is. I always got on the boat 'cos I was quick to get ashore when we came in, running the gunwales to jump out quick.'

At Park Wall Rod tells me, 'the shares were third to the boat for repairs and the nets, a third to the skipper because he made and maintained the gear all through the year, and third to the crew.' At Chickerell Hive Dennis says, 'a third of the catch went to the four owners, Ted Harman, Mac, Les Hinton and Henry Beale, then they'd also get an equal share in the shot if they'd been there at the time.' Boys got a quarter or half share of the crew share. Women took a full share, and were often part of the shot, all but Barbara and Marjorie, Chum's sisters, who went down beach most days, with Marjorie, the 'daredevil' as Barbara called her, often keeping the boat and even throwing out the seine sometimes, but Chum never included either of them in the share. Lizzie 'Ginny' Arnold at Abbotsbury fished professionally as full-time crew from her teens until well into her fifties.

Of course many fishermen remember their largest catches, when they rolled home on a high, but as Dennis Harman tells me, 'you couldn't just do it for the money as it was hard work and sometimes there were no fish. Sometimes a couple of men around about wanted to come in the shot and have a go and they came a few times but when they weren't catching, after a couple of weeks they didn't come back; hard work and no fish.' Larger catches ranged from 200 to 966 stone in May 1962. The legendary bumper catch was by Chum's Park Wall crew at 990 stone in July 1963, so great that this was only a partial landing of the full nets, some of which were cut away and lost. Dennis said that one time they watched and saw a huge rudd and assumed that they'd also launch and get a share further down, but Park Wall chanced their largest seine and somehow took the lot.

Cutting the net and 'dipping', or shovelling out fish to lighten the load so it could be hauled up, was common practice with a bumper haul. According to Dave Bartlett, 'If you got the fish out first, generally whoever chucked the net out, would what you call *keep the boat*, drift along with the boat and go off on the quarter basically to keep the fish down because the seine was in deeper water, wasn't bearing, and then come round ready to be pulled out.

But if you had a lot of fish they would rather cut and dip, or pull them out and undo the mouth of the net, the holes, and spill them out; and then spread the net back, what they call the western arm of the net, ready to put back in the boat; get the boat out, and then you'd cover up the fish and spread the other arm of the net, you know. It didn't take very long, actually; I expect... you could probably shoot every half hour, probably a little bit less if you had anyone on that knew what they were doing.'

Eventually by the 1980s, Chickerell, Park Wall and Abbotsbury crews had a tractor to assist dragging the net up a little way to empty the bunt. Dennis explains: 'The tractor had a winch on the back and two extra wheels, and that could lift out anything up to around a hundred stone weight. Anything more you'd have to cut the net and dip out. The drag did take its toll on the net.' Fishermen would make running repairs, mending the nets, or 'yarking', whilst sat out on the beach. They would do a full refit and repair over winter, knitting the net, strung between two poles, with 'yarking' needles, sometimes in the fields or in the garden.

The stern post of the lerret was used to help control landing ashore. 'The stern post had a start rope coiled on it and whoever was throwing the seine would wrap the rope around the post tight and in rough weather he'd use the drag of the net full of fish to stall the boat, so it stopped, but the crew were still rowing, and then when the rope was let out quickly at the right moment, the boat ran safely straight up the beach.' Ashore, the long end was shorter and the longer ship end took the load. It was this ship end that the younger crew, jumping out of the boat, took up to heave over their shoulders. They walked up the steep beach, arm over arm of net rolled tight into a rope, then ran around to the back once their rope was slack to walk further down the steep and heave over the shoulder again.

blue green tiger-stripes,
delicious oily fish
mackerel skies tide a weather

Once the catch was ashore, the mackerel were either wetted on hessian sacks to keep them fresh or dug into nests on the beach whilst the crew shot again. The mackerel was sorted into sizes – small, medium and large – and weighed. There was a large pair of weighing scales with a two-stone weight on the beach. The fish were then packed into crates or boxes and punted or 'quanted' across the Fleet and loaded onto the cart or truck. In older times, fish were not even weighed. Rab remembers: 'When I started, first of all the fish were counted. You'd have three men round, usually the old men, and they'd pick up four, eight twelve... when they got to a hundred they'd chuck a fish out, that was the "tally fish". We'd share the tally fish, that's what the boys would take home. Quite a few tally fish home in several thousand fish there.' Dennis says, 'Sometimes you'd be packing the large ones and there wasn't quite enough and they'd hide a few smaller below the top, they all did it.'

Chesil fishermen fished to supplement their income for many generations. The bounty was shared and the fish was necessary summer and winter; 'we lived off mackerel back then.' A pioneering, resourceful spirit is part of the coastal tradition, essential to survival of rural winters, taking opportunity as it comes. *The London Journal* recorded in 1752 that 'all the people of Abbotsbury, including the Vicar, are thieves, smugglers and plunderers of wrecks,' but this might have applied to any rural coastal village along British shores. Necessity. There was a sea-change shift from subsistence to profit in the fishing after the Wars. And more than any of them, it was the likes of Chummy Northover and Ash Huddy whose particular blend of fearlessness, talent, energy and luck made them good leaders, fishermen and entrepreneurs, relentless in their passion for seining and business.

Chummy recorded his fine-pencilled accounts and ledgers with lists of the crews involved, the crew list transcribed by Rod at the back of this book. Chum wrote in pages of old recipe books belonging to Aunt May (Uncle George's wife) or even in the back of old school exercise books belonging to Rex and Rod (his nephews); he used whatever paper was available. All of these he stored at Uncle George's cottage on a pantry shelf near the hearth amongst Aunt May's pans, teapot and saucers. Most seine captains burned their books on retiring.

'It was all pound notes,' Edward Marshallsay remembers, 'you got paid monthly and what I think he (Chum) done, you got paid for the mackerel. What he used to do then, three maybe four days before Christmas, long after the fishing was over, there would be

The Park Wall crew with catch on beach.

Park Wall using slings for a large catch to cut the net and dip out. Left to right: Charl Legg, Johnny Randall, Donald Peach, Chum.

a tap at the door and it was Chummy with an envelope, and this was the extra money he'd kept back for the other fish, not tonnes of them but mullet, squid, a few bass here and there, things like that.'

I ask why the accounts were hidden, and we will never know for sure. All the seine business was cash. There was a lot of cash involved. Teams were not employed in the conventional sense; they were part-timers with other jobs, responsible for their own stamp cards. Most seined nights as the 'tea-time' crew and weekends. The accounts were to keep track of the many different crews and for Chummy, Ash, Henry, Mac or Louis to square up shares for each shot, but perhaps not with the tax man, though Greenslade fish merchant figures all went through the books. Rab tells us that on Portland he was not allowed to take photos of the catches; ''owd man, he wouldn't have it.' Rab had a camera, other gadgets, and even bought his own boat after a year with seining money. Edward Marshallsay bought two motorbikes. Chummy invested in properties, campsites and land. Alan says that if anyone asked about your catches you'd say 'few to eat, few to sell.' You'd never tell anybody what was caught, there was as little trace as a sea path, the actual numbers and figures swallowed in the wake of the sea.

'We fished most evenings,' says Dennis. 'Monday, Tuesday, Wednesday, Thursday and Sundays, not Fridays or Saturdays as there was no market. There was no market Sundays so you had the Fridays and Saturdays off, and if the catches were large with the other two Fleet crews, the buyers might stop the fishermen, or ask for only one tonne. If all the teams at Chickerell, Park Wall and, later, Moonfleet had been catching well and taken three shots over three days early in the week, this might happen, they might tell you to stop as they couldn't take any more.'

Net sizes and dimensions were also hush hush. We do have notes of Chum's big and little seine and the sizes seem to vary from catch to catch as he was tweaking them. The largest was big – '62 feet in the bunt', as Dave Bartlett remembers. George Randall used to make the Park Wall seines, with basic net purchased from Gundry in Bridport. Rab tells me about 'loat' sections of net sewn together, each with narrower meshes to trap the fish. The drop from the beach is deeper in Portland and less deep towards Abbotsbury, dictating the size of the seines. There was often a cork tied to the middle of the bunt so that the crews walking the arms ashore had an idea of where the centre of the bag lay in the tide.

In April, Ash Huddy came up to Park Wall and Wyke, and from May to August the Park Wall, Chickerell, Wyke and Langton crews moved down to Abbotsbury. There was some elastic to the territory, but understandings may have been based on tolerance and old family connections. There were incidents over competitive grounds. One time when Park Wall missed a catch, older crew blamed the youngsters (including Rod) who were messing about on the beach. Chum consequently banned Rod and two friends from beach for three months. Luckily, Aunt Gwen (Chum's sister) intervened for Rod ('she sort of ruled Chum in a way') and this ban was reduced to a month; 'you didn't cross Uncle Chum.'

Other incidents resulted in the throwing of pebbles back in the day. Edward tells me about the time when Harold Parker, who fished with Chum, also had a small net and a private buyer for his catches, which caused resentment. He went out one time and shot a small seine, and Chummy shot a large seine over the top and may have cut Harold's net. This is how Ken Gowans, who was rowing with Harold that day, remembers it: 'We got there first just before Chummy did. Well. What happened next, we went round them (the fish). Chummy Northover made his boat go across our seine and tried to drive them (the fish) out. Bedlam it was. Harold Parker had the oar and was swinging his oar over at Chummy.' There was a complaint, and an official inquiry investigated by The Fisheries Department. Stones may have been thrown. Anyway, Chum got off with a fine and made an apology. There are many more stories like this, many others lost.

skid down the beach for them,
ride out the surf,
splsh-pfly, oars in, 'pull hard'!

5

The folk lerret

Chesil was divided into fishing territories for lerret companies and these inshore fishing grounds were highly competitive, but you could live off the yield of a small open working boat with able hands in times of want. When I talk to seine families it sounds as if there was hardship in rural villages by the sea until relatively recent times.

Old Dorset seine traditions were preserved owing to the physical demands of beach and its lee shore (during the prevailing southwesterlies), making it a daunting prospect for outsiders and passing ships on merchant routes through Lyme Bay and Portland Roads, and unsuitable for large craft and engines. The lerret was non-motorised, and the only boat design safe and adequate for rougher launches and landings, making it possible for crews to row out and work the seine in challenging conditions. Whilst lighter square-back seiners were preferred by crews for calm seas all along the Chesil in living memory, the lerret, which had been retired elsewhere, was still in use much later at Langton and Park Wall, essential in order to get out and return safely in heavy surf.

The lerret boat is part of an older Chesil language – part Dorset, part Mediterranean. Its design evolution is probably a throwback to the busy maritime ports of Weymouth and Portland where technical news and advances might be imparted by passing seafarers and adopted. In *The Lerrets of Chesil Bank* (1977), Eric Mckee followed Royal Navy Commander Kerr in dating the lerret with 'three hundred years behind her,' though it likely evolved from earlier craft on the Continent and developed from Fleetwater trow designs. The most popular legend has the origins of the name

Opposite: The Avalanche and *Forest* rescue in lerrets by local fishermen in 1877 (from the Portland Museum Collection).

Putting the seine net back into the lerret *Silver Star*: Ted Harman, Chappie Beale, Sid Peach, Les Hinton and Jonathan (courtesy of Dennis Harman).

deriving from a Portland boat called *The Lady of Loretto*, built sometime before 1682 when it was gifted in a will, one merchant Captain having visited Ancona where he was impressed by a striking gold-gilded statue of the Virgin.

Like any good folk story or song, the lerret was crafted to cross centuries of currents alive in hands and voices, its form developed through function and use, and passed down from boat-builder to boat-builder with hardly a written note or drawing to formalise exact dimensions. This is how the old wooden boats were built, alive to the shifts of the beach and fishermen's modifications. Local boat-builders knew lerret shapes and patterns by eye as a doctor may know the human body. None was the same. Each had its own truth and mystery.

That said, Steve Matthews, a Weymouth builder and former boat-builder, points out: 'They weren't trying to build racing yachts. What fishermen wanted was cheap, functioning boats and they cut corners asking for length off to save money ... Ron Berry would

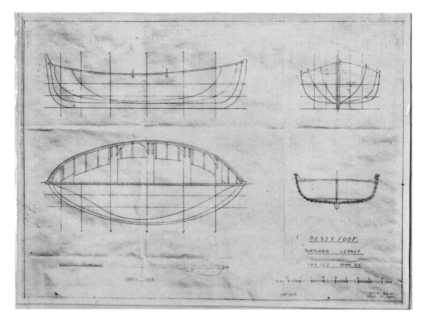

An order for *Pussy Foot* – a 17ft lerret – made of elm (from the Weymouth Museum Collection).

build a flat-back in ten days on his own, or a week with help.'

There are three types of boat native to Chesil: the lerret and the square-back or square-sterned rowing boat are both seaworthy, and the flat-bottomed trow is rowed across the Fleet or punted with a quant or pole through the shallows. You had to cross the Fleet from Chickerell Hive and Park Wall in a trow to get to the farside beach where seine boats rested on the crest. Then you had to launch the lerret and fish, return the same way with the fish, and finally get the fish to the road or lorry. 'It was crazy really the amount of effort it all took,' remembers Mike Beale, who seined in the Chickerell crew with his father, Henry Beale. The loaded trow was punted from the stern with a pole in the shallows – the rower could stand with amidships stacked high with boxes.

Rod's personal library of maritime and Dorset histories, together with documents in the Dorset library archives and McKee's *Working Boats of Britain* repeat key facts about lerret, larrit, larrotte or lerritt lore that have weathered the centuries. It is a surf boat, a wide and sturdy row boat with a flat floor that you can stand up in, or throw out a heavy net from, with wide-flared curves that pinch in at the ends. The bow and stern post double-ends are crucially balanced for buoyancy and bearing so that in cross-currents offshore, and when launching or returning to the steep shingle incline, the boat lifts onto the beach for the landing without the risk of a low back flooded by the next wave, and without the danger of swinging 'broadside' into the following waves as they dump down onto it, which might swamp or turn it over before it can be pulled to safety.

Such stability meant the lerret was useful as a lifeboat, for salvage of cargo from wrecks, and for free-trading. The lerret traditionally had eight, six or four oars, the larger lerrets carried lug mainsail and sprit mizzen mast. Larger seiners of up to 21 feet were used in smuggling days to sail as far as Alderney and back in a night. Larger lerrets persisted mainly at the Portland end of Chesil and required even more hands to launch and recover. Two six-oared lerrets famously rescued survivors of the ships *Avalanche* and *Forest* in 1877, inspiring an RNLI lerret prototype that was supplied but never adopted on Portland owing to lack of enthusiasm by local fishermen. They weren't adverse to courageous rescue, but preferred their ancient manorial salvage rights of wreck to the RNLI rules, willing to rescue as they had always done, using the boats they knew would handle the sea without additional modifications. There is a rich tradition of fishermen serving as volunteer Auxiliary Coastguards along Chesil, where there were numerous stations, now all gone.

The smaller, four-oared lerret, 16–19 feet in length with a beam of up to 7 feet (width), was favoured from the mid-twentieth century, and the lighter and shorter square-stern row boats were also widely used, and continue to be used to nip in and out of the beach with small seines and pots, and fewer hands.

Rab talks to me about the longevity of one of his old flat-sterned boats, sold on and still afloat at Ferry Bridge. 'I brought up one of Joey's old boats, the *229*. Built in 1839 it was, used to have a box keel for sail but that was long gone. Hardly anything in him

Park Wall launch.

Chiswell, Portland, in 1900 (from the Portland Museum Collection).

Chickerell Hive crew load boxes of mackerel from the trow to give to the buyer (courtesy of Dennis Harman).

The Farn Family and their lerret *Pleasure*, 1935 (from the Portland Museum Collection). This boat was later sold to Chummy.

original, all changed as each plank cracked, it was all replaced. I don't think there was anything original in it. It was an excellent sea boat. Excellent. When we had that gale in 1974, terrible sea. I was all summer repairing it. I can recall it had two holes, I could've crawled right through the boat. I mended it in the fishing store. Took me ages, thwarts [seats], gunwales, planking. A proper beach boat. Low and similar to the lerret if you put two ends on it. Cut in. Same shapes.'

The trows are flat-bottomed, double-ended or square-transomed boats, around 17 feet long, that sit low in the waters of the Fleet. Traditionally made of elmwood with mahogany thwarts, many are now fibreglass. The Estate still uses trows for shooting wildfowl in the backwater.

On enquiry at Weymouth Museum, I discover that only one artefact survives from all of the many boat-builders in Weymouth and Wyke: a 1934 receipt from J. M. Wills, based at Ferry Bridge where the Crab Shack now stands, for Fred Farn's new lerret (no oars) at £20. Lerret oars are shaped as 'copsea' oars. Copsea is a flat, pear-shaped plank attached to the loom, with a hole on it which slips over the thole pin and a small oar blade. The oar can't catch a crab with this set-up, and if you stand up and move around, or even beach the boat, the oars sit steady and do not fall out of the pins. As far as I understand it, the thole pin can take a great load with minimal wear.

Roll call of lerrets known and gone. All the miles, seapaths, mackerel slinks and rusty-poled years, sometimes more audible in stillness. It is never still out there. Let Chesil do the talking once the geese have settled down.

On a sparkly day in early January, Don takes me out in a fibreglass blue-and-white trow (borrowed from local eel fisherman Gary Downton) to go over to the rudge at Moonfleet. I test out the double midships copsea oars for myself on the way home. As we head back after our adventures, the northwesterly picks up with slight wave crests curling up to the sound of two hundred geese honking on a fly-by as the tide runs out of the lagoon. I certainly struggle to hold our course, though it is not far at this point to get straight across. With almost-palm-blisters from gripping the oars to get a long and strong pull, we cross the main width of the channel back to Moonfleet Manor, where this trow belongs. In the middle of the Fleet, joy and excitement in the dance of wavelets and slurp of insistent water slapping the hull, the betwixt and between, the Jurassic glimpses, the relative shelter of the ridge and the roar of what lies beyond it. There is a 'float-me' lure to the charm of this Fleet-in-Wonderland.

Lerret- and trow-builders remembered in living memory include Derek Andrews, Ron Berry, Nobby and Tim Clark, Paul Meers, Bert Merrit, Royston Mowlem, Percy Roberts, Joseph Talbot of Weymouth and Jack Wills of Ferry Bridge. *Christina* (WH289) was the last lerret working on Portland and was owned by P. Brown. Gail McGarva built the first lerret for over forty years in 2011 (*see* page 179). Called *Littlesea*, it is now the only seaworthy lerret on the Chesil Beach, and is recognised as an official replica by National Historic Ships and listed on their Register.

Of the lerrets listed in Appendix 4, *Silver Star* (registered at Weymouth as WH600) has been saved from rot by Don Moxom and David Carter of Portland Museum. Since the 2000s, it has been displayed in Portland Museum garden, Chesil Heritage Centre and Abbotsbury Tithe Barn, and currently sits on the hard outside the Castletown D-Day Centre on Portland. It is *Silver Star* that Dennis and Sandra's fathers seined at Chickerell Hive. The syndicate had bought the boat from Fred Randall at Wyke Regis in the 1950s. The seine companies bought and sold, repaired and wintered lerrets. Mike Beale tells me that *Silver Star* was then completely refitted and planked in the 1960s by Ron Berry. We will never know how many times it was launched for seining since its construction in 1913 – hundreds of times a summer, perhaps for eighty years.

In a recording of Betty Dalley in 2011, Betty mentions a lerret pulled up and left on the beach at Abbotsbury and almost destroyed by tourists sitting in and rocking it. Possibly Ash Huddy's lerrets *Jubilee* and then *Queen Mary* met the same end. *Vera* and *Chesil*

David Bartlett punting a trow (photo by Pauline Rook).

Relaunch of six-oared lerret, *Christina*, WH289 (courtesy of the Portland Museum Collection).

Queen had been built side by side by Jack Wills at Ferry Bridge in 1923. Betty explains how she came to be a fisherwoman: 'During the war the men all got called up and so we used to go and help, my sisters and the ones that were left. That's how it came to be.' Betty seined as a young woman, and her sister Lizzie remained a professional fisherwoman all of her life. 'She was out there and throwing the seine well into her sixties,' Pete Stevens tells me, 'and Ash Huddy used to be fishing daylight to dark.'

Following ancient custom, lerrets to the present day have a 'hag stone' or 'holy stone' (a holed pebble), tied to the ringbolt in the bows. The start rope (or 'painter') is threaded through the stone for luck, 'to keep away witches' and to bring safe passage at sea. Pete Stevens also mentions other superstitions widely followed by his company at Abbotsbury including not wearing green. I've heard this mariner's superstition before, but there was one I hadn't... when an Abbotsbury priest came down to meet the fishermen wearing glasses he was told it was bad luck for the crew to go out after seeing this sight.

From Rab: 'Well we always considered that a pebble with a hole in him was a lucky pebble, and that would bring you good luck... I mean, still now, my son's got one hanging in his boat; he's got it tied onto the fore; we got one hanging in the store, probably got one out the back yard. When he was very small, when I say very small, he might have been six or something like that because both boys spent their life on the beach – they were always down there fishing off the rocks and generally messing about – and I told him one day, when we were down there, and I showed him a pebble with a hole in it, and I told him it was a lucky pebble. That was all right. And a couple of days later he came home in the afternoon, and he had a job to keep his trousers up, he had so many pebbles with holes in, in his pockets, that his trousers would hardly – he had to hold his trousers up, and his pockets were all bulging with pebbles. Lucky boy. And he's still fishing.'

Betty remembered how during the war seine fishing continued, sometimes with dogfights going on overhead. Barnes Wallis tested out the prototype of the bouncing bomb between Moonfleet House and New Barn, and beach was guarded by Special Constables and closed off except for defences, access for those living in the coastguard cottages, and fishermen. In Abbotsbury, after Julia Arnold heard how her daughters were treated working in service as maids, she sent for them to come home so that they could go to beach and fish with the older men who had stayed back from fighting, all on Huddy's crew, to earn a living. Ash sometimes used to say, 'we've a boat full of walking sticks,' according to Betty Dalley.

The traditional start of the seine season was Good Friday on Portland, and a prize of a gallon of beer was offered from Devenish Brewery for the first mackerel of the season. Further down Chesil from Abbotsbury, Swyre and Burton, the season officially started on Garland Day on 13th May when huge flower garlands were made in the village and walked down to the sea as an offering to bless and bring luck to the fishing boats. Garland days were festive rituals, days of singing, dancing and hurdy-gurdy chords, such customs dying out by the mid-nineteenth century, although the making of garlands was carried on by Julia and then Betty Dalley until Betty's death.

II

Voices of Chesil Beach

The following pages are based on oral history interviews, with transcripts selected from longer recordings. These literal transcripts are presented with as little editing as possible to give a feel for the rhythm, expression and emphasis of dialect. Quotations are also attributed throughout the book to transcripts taken from Gail McGarva's oral history recordings, made in 2011.

Ash Huddy's hut on Abbotsbury beach 150 yards along from the red-brick coastguards' (no longer there). Top left to right: Gabriel Arnold (standing), Ash Huddy, Fred Roper, Shep Arnold, Spot the dog, Ashley Arnold, Scrummy Roper and Lizzie Arnold (courtesy of Alan Arnold).

ROD CONDLIFFE
Nephew of Chum ('Chummy') Northover, fisherman with the Park Wall crew.

CELIA HARRISON:
Cousin of Rod, daughter of Boyce, Chum's brother.

REX IRELAND
Cousin of Rod, son of Marjorie, Chum's sister.

JACKIE IRELAND
Wife of Rex Ireland.

EDWARD MARSHALLSAY
Fisherman with the Park Wall crew.

RICHARD & DAVID LARCOMBE
Brothers who fished with their father on *Yogi Bear* from West Bay.

DAVE BARTLETT
Fisherman at Abbotsbury and Park Wall (recordings 2011 from Gail McGarva's archive).

IAN REEDER
Fisherman at Langton Herring (recordings 2011 from Gail McGarva's archive).

BETTY & DICK DALLEY
Seiners at Abbotsbury (recordings 2011 from Gail McGarva's archive).

DON MOXOM
Former Fleet warden to the Earl of Ilchester, Fleet historian.

DAVID CARTER
Local historian and trustee at Portland Museum.

RAB STONE
Quarryman, fisherman, beachcomber, gardener and artist.

ALAN ARNOLD
Fisherman on Ash Huddy's crew, Abbotsbury.

PETE STEVENS
Fisherman with Ash Huddy, Alan's cousin.

STEVE MATTHEWS
Builder, boat builder and former fisherman, Weymouth.

DENNIS HARMAN
Fisherman of Chickerell Hive crew with brother, Barry, and father, Ted.

SANDRA FRETWELL
Daughter of Henry 'Chappie' Beale, fisherman of Chickerell Hive crew.

MIKE BEALE
Fished with father Henry Beale.

PAT DONNELLY
Fisherman on Ash Huddy's crew, Abbotsbury.

PETE PARSON
Fisherman, Burton Bradstock.

PHIL HUTCHINGS
Fisherman, Burton Bradstock.

PAT HUTCHINGS
Phil's wife, and Desi Gape's daughter.

NANCY GAPE
Wife of fisherman, Desmond ('Desi') Gape, Burton Bradstock.

RICKY GAPE
Fisherman at Burton Hive Beach and Desi Gape's son.

6

Portland

Rab Stone (b. 1940)

I started fishing when I could pull an oar and carry a fish basket with about four stone of fish, that would be about thirteen years old. I'd come home from school at lunchtime and come out over Lankeridge at the old Priory Corner, out over that ridge path with steps at the top goin' down to Killick's Hill. Lots of times I'd gone out over that edge and the mackerel boats just pushin' off. They'd have a shot, the boat out with the crew and I never went home. I'd miss dinner entirely and carry fish home in the school clothes. Mother washed the uniform only once a week. 'You made'm like it boy,' she'd say, 'you'll 'ave to go to school in 'em tomorrow,' and several of the girls complained I smelt. The mackerel all runned down your back, see, and I did smell. 'He smells,' they'd say, and they made me sit at the back of the class.

Joey Stone practically brought me up but he wasn't my biological father. They used to call him 'The Crow', but not to his face. He was terrible sometimes. The last man to chew tobacco on Portland. Wasn't allowed to chew 'home or out with his wife, but he would chew when he was at the fishing. All the time. First thing he used to do when he'm out the house in the morning was cut himself a plug and he'd chew all day and the last thing he did at night was spit the plug out. Not the same one. We'd be off there fishing and the weather might be quite rough, you know, quite lumpy, and he'd

Opposite: Rab Stone feathering for mackerel (courtesy of Rab Stone).

Seine Boat on top of the beach at Chiswell, Portland (from the Portland Museum Collection).

say, 'Do you want a chew, boy, have a bit o' this, I took the sting out of it.' 'No thanks, Joe,' I'd say, and he'd laugh.

Joey didn't come back for you, oh no. When the long arm come ashore, they used to shout 'All strangers let go!' If you weren't in the shot you had to let go then.

His father died of pneumonia after being run down off in the boat. There was a feud going at the time, there was a feud and somebody ran him down and he went into the water, caught pneumonia. That's what killed 'im.

Joey used to say, 'Don't ever start a war down here, son,' he said. 'Worse thing you can ever do. If you want to have anybody,' he said, 'you wait 'til they're off and 'tis bad weather, shuffy' – that's that long drag you get on the rollers, they come in and when they pitch you get the long drag and up and back again, then the next big roller, that's what they call shuffy weather. 'You just wait 'til we got a shuff and they want to come ashore and you walk away and leave them, that's the way you 'ave 'em. No need to start a war. If they're off with one hand, all's you've got to do's walk away.' Because you only had the other fishermen to get you ashore.

Rab Stone and Dave Huddy ('Chiefy') in their boat *We Dree*. In the first year they rowed everywhere and made enough money to buy a small seagull engine (courtesy of Rab Stone).

I don't remember a lerret rigged for sail and only one seine boat; all the rest were lost by the time I started fishing. Some years after Joe retired from full-time fishing I took on his old boat *WH229* which had a box keel for sailing which was taken out in the mid-1950s, knocked about in a gale and I repaired it. Before you had the outboard engine, couple of the blokes I fished with, Wobbler Anthony (he had one leg longer than the other), him and a couple of other blokes, they used to row up 'Stennas' [off Budmouth Academy school in Chickerell] three-handed, so the man in the bow had two oars and then the two men amidships with an oar each. Me father-in-law said to me one time, he said, 'We've rowed up Stennas.' Now mind, you'd row up four times to haul one trot. You'd row up, shoot it, row home. Then row up the next day, haul um, then row home again. 'Rowed all up Stennas,' he'd said, 'and we never had a fish.' Stennas was a fishing mark, something to do with Steine house, I'm not sure where Steine House was actually. Think that was it. Other mark was Smillage. I don't know where that was. Lot of the fishing knowhow about the fishing grounds and marks had gone by the time I got there.

Lerret, *Sunday at Home*, Church Ope (from the Portland Museum Collection).

Rab and crew spratting off Chesil, September 1989. Inside the boat Rab on oars, Georgie Boatswain throwing the net. Rab's son, Ian Stone, is the last man on the rope nearest the camera (courtesy of Rab Stone).

There was only two mackerel crews and Rats' crew never came down much past Cove House. When I say a mackerel crew that is to say manned and owned by entirely different people. We had three boats so we had three crews, see, but it was all known as one crew. Rats Allen and Rats' father, they had another crew. Bricks Stone used to throw the net. I remember Rats. He died on the beach. I was there. We was pulling up planks and large timbers that were washed ashore. I was still at school. Rats was there and at that time quite a lot of fishermen, and they said, 'Rats is down, we'll go over and have a look in a bit.' By the time they got over he was dead.

We worked from Station Holler, down this way, just past Cove House, up as far as the beginning of the Fleet. That span of beach we worked wherever we happened to be. At one time they had three lerrets. If you had a dozen men to a lerret, that was a crew of three dozen, thirty-odd men, could've been more. A crew, you see, consisted mostly of men who knew the beach 'cos when you launched a boat, launched a lerret, the men on the oars and the man that threw the net were already sat in the boat. You had to have the rest of the crew to launch it. The ones that launched it was just as important, if not more important, than the men sat in the boat. You had to be able to judge the sea. We used to go out in quite rough weather, so the men on the beach were just as important, like when they went off and got the crew and one or two passengers off the wrecks, *Avalanche* and *Forest*, after collision, they only named the men in the boat afterwards in all the papers. If you didn't have a good crew on the shore, them men in the boat wouldn't have got out there or got back. They had to be on the shore and you had to gauge the sea when you pulled the boat in, you had to gauge the sea otherwise they'd tip the boat up and drown 'em. You had to have someone there to say, 'Now's the time, pull!' Practically everybody that worked it knew the beach. Very few newcomers. They wouldn't have taken part in anything like that.

Much later, visitors came. Joey said never to pick a fight with other fishermen but it was different with visitors. Would've been a riot if they'd got in the way. Stone through the bottom of the boat. If someone was vindictive it wasn't unheard of that someone might put an ashlar (a large stone block) through another one's hull. Joey would say, 'Don't never start a war, young un, 'cos you don't know where it'll end.'

Everybody that was there when the boat put the westered end of the net ashore had a share [of the fish]. If you got there later, you mightn't get a share. You had to throw a pebble in the basket. I fished with Rats one time and I threw a pebble in the basket, and he threw mine out. I weren't very old. 'You're only a boy,' he said. 'I carried those bloody mackerel, and I get a share up west,' I said. He said, 'You in't up west now.' 'That's the last time I fish 'ere,' I said. Joey never fished Saturday, there being no market on Sunday. Rats did. They shot and I thought, 'Bugger, Rats is having a shot,' and got hold of the rope and carried the baskets. I did get a share of the fish, but no money. All the crews put a basket of fish aside to share out later, so we all went home with a feed, and if my share was more than mother needed, I'd sell the rest on my way home at three old pence each.

The [fish merchant's] lorry came anywhere up the beach road. Hanney, they had a shop over Weymouth, Hanney Brothers. The only time we ever had Greenslades round here was if Hanney didn't want it. He always had first shout. He came in every day for the crab and lobster and we'd call him and he'd drive the lorry over with the boxes on for all the mackerel. Someone would have to walk down to the Ferrybridge Inn to phone and he'd pick them up on the way with a crate of beer. They'd put it on the night train to London and it'd be in Billingsgate when it opened four o'clock in the morning. They weren't gutted. Weren't even iced down. We never had ice or nothing like that, no ice-making machine. The lorry'd drive up onto the station platform and stack the boxes in the truck. Those were the days when women shopped every day, nothing kept for long.

Rab and the boys, Martin to his left, home from sea in the merchant navy, and Ian to his right (photo by George Wright).

Sometimes mother would souse them [the mackerel] poached with vinegar and a bay leaf, but nearly always fried. Lovely, still love them. Christ, we used to live on them long ago. When the mackerel were there in greatest numbers we never used to take bait out for fishing crab, used catch enough on the way out to bait all your pots and enough for tea. This is no word of lie – one time a feller wanted five stone of mackerel, around the time when chest freezers came in and people had 'em at home, and so we pushed the boat out, went out the back of the moorings, filled the basket, had five stone, pulled the boat back on the beach again, half an hour.

Many's the time I'd go and see how the nippers were going on selling by the roadside, and they'd be running low, so one of the boys and me, we'd go and push the boat in, have four or five stone, row shore, put the fish by the side of the road and sell them and go back an hour later and do it again if the tide was good.

August mackerel were often smaller and fatter, 'Haymakers' or 'Harvest Mackerel' they were called. Used to sort 'em in crocks to eat for winter, salt the mackerel, dried them off. The crock was a pot glazed in the inside, not the outside. You cut the mackerel down the back, top and tail them, then you rub salt over them. When fairly dry you used to pack them in the crock laid out flat, that way, then that way, then that way. Pack 'em until the crock was full up, put a layer of salt between every layer of fish. As the salt took the moisture out the fish you'd drain the pot – 'tip the jipper down the gutter, boy' – and you'd go out the store and tip the jipper through the pebbles, and perhaps you'd have to pack some more salt on. Hard as boards if you did it right, oily brown jipper it was. They'd last all winter. Then you'd put them in fresh water to get the salt out of them. Salt mackerel and potatoes was your staple diet here you see, for winter, lovely.

I loved the fishing, could think of nothing else from junior school. Used to get sick sometimes. Hot thundery sweaty weather, bad weather. If I was rough, Joey used to make me row. He used to say, 'Take your mind off it, boy, keep your head up in the air. If you want to go ashore you'n bloody get out an' walk, you bide there and row.' He wasn't going to drop me off on a ledge, so I bided there and I rowed like he said. We were off Bill Point at that time, waiting for the tide to ease so we could haul the crab pots. They'd fish about eighty to ninety pots all b'hand every day that was fit. We used to pray for bad weather now and then to go up the allotment. Most of the fishermen had an allotment.

We used to have a couple of size seines. Sometimes in September or October if it was really calm we used to go out 'timming'. We'd put the net in the seine boat and go down at the night-time, started off around six or seven, about high water, and shoot not too far off, just shoot round and haul it ashore and we'd catch mullet and bass and whiting and you'd fill two baskets. You'd put them back in the store and shoot again. Up as far as Cove House. You might have six shots at night in the dark. Go on home by eight or nine and the fish left in the store for the buyer in the morning. I've got a picture at home, not that long ago, when we shot for sprats in the morning. Three tonne we had. Took us most of the day to get them up Brandy Row for the buyer to pick up.

Joey used to say to me and Fishy [Fishy's real name was Brian Newton; he went to school with Rab and they both fished in Joey Stone's crew], 'You want to put a bit of trot off, a long line, boy, you'd going to put a net off?' and we'd say, 'Yes, Joe, but we ain't got a net.' And he'd show us how to make them up. You have a long line and then you cut traces (3ft 6"). You'd lose six inches tying them on three foot apart. You'd tie the trace on the main beam and on the end of the trace you tie a hook, you'd put two hooks together and stretch out and that was where the next one was tied on. They'd never catch up again 'cos they were just too far apart to reach. We might have three hundred hooks at six foot apart, you might have a mile of trot down.

The winter of 1963 when Rab was working in the quarries and they were stood off six or seven weeks due to cold. Rab's crew spent their time netting mullet. Left to right, back: Joey Stone, Doc Smith, Mouse Coleman and Norman Comben. Front: Vic Hayes, Billy Wills, Rab, Bob White and Rich Carter just out of shot (courtesy of Rab Stone).

Every so many hooks we'd put a barrel lead on. We made our own leads. You'd thread them on, then tie them at either end and make sure the rope stayed on the bottom. All depended on how much bait you had. Made them in lengths and tied the long ends together. Mackerel bait. We never fished until the autumn for trots. We didn't fish until the mackerel prices went down, and then you could afford to use them for bait on the hooks. Joey'd say, 'This is the knot to use to tie the hook on, this is the rolling hitch for the trace, go and stretch it, this is how you stretch it, but don't stretch it on the top of the beach 'cos it'll only go and put ideas in them bugger's heads that ain't got any ideas,' so you had to do it where others wouldn't see.

Portland.   Chesil Beach & General View.

Lerrets pulled up on 'the winter curb' at Portland (postcard from Rab's collection).

Winter time was make and mend. The nets were bark cotton. In the winter you'd have a day and you'd have the stove going; we had one of they 'Slow be Sures'. We used to make all our gear, leads and corks. We had a mobile anvil and we made the leads. Now it's woven into the line. In those days we'd melt lead and then we'd put them in the mould and knock them out in the stone hut. Upstairs they'd make and stretch the nets. Downstairs was where they made the pots and stacked them up. In the next store was a copper for barking the nets and one day each winter, 'whorf', our old man used to say, 'tomorrow morning' and we used to get there early to light the stove. It was built of a big stone with a hole in the middle for the fire 'cos you used to bark a load at a time and that was quite big. Bark came in sacks and we boiled it up. Put the net in. We barked 'cos you didn't want the fish to strike the net. If you left it white they might run into it. You wanted them to go down into the hose. You'd bark a load at a time but when you got to the bunt and hose it was enormous. Our bunt and hose fished 62 feet deep. You think of that, top to bottom 'cos it had to touch the bottom, he couldn't let them out underneath and he couldn't let them out over the top and the water is deep down here at our end of the beach. In the winter, if it was calm, we went gill netting, and if it was rough there was beach combing, for wood mostly or whatever was washing up.

Aish Huddy [some fishermen who remember him, still speak of Ash as 'Aish'] used to put the boat on a three-tonne lorry and he'd come down to Portland. News would get round that the fish turned up. You could look all the way up the beach from Chesil, and the old men would be sitting along the beach and one fellow would say, 'Abbotsbury men's down… Chickerell men's down… come on then boys,' and they'd all launch. There was always someone on the beach at all times, always someone looking out.

A dockeryard matey at that time might be on seven pounds a week or less, but might get three pounds share on a decent shot, and if you got three shots in the week… you've more than doubled your wages like that. All cash. Joey Stone used to keep two books – one official, one secret. He was brilliant with figures. He'd just run his finger across the numbers in his book and tot it all up, just like that.

You growed up very young. You'd get a smack on the ear if you stepped out. Fellers used to shout at us and swear. I was always polite – you see'd what happened to the other boys – so I went up one evening and they was all by the boat sitting on a jacket with a net up the boat ready to go, and 'wazer's up'. One would watch at the back of the boat whilst the others played cards and I walked up the beach and said, 'Evening Mr Huddy. Where's David today?' I said, and he only hit me over the head he did.

The men sat there in all weathers, playing Euchre. They'd all chat what was happening in the village. I'd sit on the end of the stick as a nipper and listen and you'd never know, if you sat there and behaved yourself you might get a go, you might get out on the boat. You had to behave yourself, seen and not heard was the rule of the day, too damned right. 'Cos we were nippers we used to get excited and shout, japes and all sorts.

But you sat round and talked to people in those days, no television, nothing to pass the time, so all the old men would be out all summer. All the old places and walls. Uncle Sunny (Albert Saunders) was there all year round. He had a store and it was chocker-full and there was a stove at the back and the gear was all packed up all around to the rafters. He had a boat that was presented to him when the wreck of the Admiralty trawler, the *James Fennel*, came ashore this side of Blacknor. Sunny'd saved all sixteen crew. There was a lot of talk with ideas of what he was out there for. There was a medal and a collection. They presented him with the seine boat, they towed him in the boat through the streets and people threw money in the boat and this is what bought all the gear and nets. That's how he got his boat. He'd been on the wooden sailing boats, square-riggers. He was an old seaman, couldn't read.

Sunny was everyone's uncle. Uncle Sunny… we would come shore with some fish and he'd say, 'You've been off the Dutchman, do you know the marks?' and we'd say, 'No, Uncle. So you know the marks, Uncle?' and he'd say, 'Ah well, there you are'… and he wouldn't tell us the marks. Being nippers, we didn't take any marks. We just fished and then we packed it in and came home. He used to fish on his own. He had trot gear off and a bloody great sharbit 120 pound or more, hundred weight. A single skate. He couldn't get un in the boat so put another hook into un and rowed um back. Fishy would go off with Uncle. I never did. He used to say, 'It's the ebb sets skewer', and if you catch it at the right time you can see those rollers and they come in at an angle up the beach, they don't come in straight, 'that's the ebb sets skewer, son,' and I'd say, 'Bugger, he's having me on half the time.'

You were around the men and they weren't that old really, only from their forties to sixties most of 'em, but when you were twelve or fifteen they were quite old. Left school at fifteen and worked in the quarries and fished as well. You learned on the beach. By the time my own boys were old enough to fish, things had changed. Seine had finished in the early 1970s for us, all finished by then.

Lerrets all left out. You have to look after the wooden boats and scrape them down and linseed oil then varnish – that elm, if it dried out, became brittle, and I've seen elm planks crack up and down that way. Varnished every year, scraped for the first years, just the flakes off, but every third year took them down to the wood, took everything off. Three lerrets, seven boats all together had to be scraped and varnished every year. In the Fleet the seine boats would be pulled into the water to soak up the water to swell. We never did that, never had to plim up, we kept 'em oiled and varnished.

Fishing was secret, you didn't shout about it. Fish at any one time, there's a limit. Today, tomorrow, or this season. You had to share it with half a dozen people fishing in the same place. Part of it was about the nets and how you put it together, and that was not common knowledge, it was a skill. Mousey Coleman, he used to do our nets but all that was in his head, it was all in his head and that was of great value. Others didn't have the skill. No records though. Big seine was sixty- or eighty-foot deep, I remember the old fella, Joey, saying, but we haven't got the records. You'd need the records to build the nets again for the depths.

They'd say, 'If you have a lot of rain the rivers'll flood,' and there might be salmon. Should've gone back to Abbotsbury, nearest river that ran into the bay, but they never did. Worth a lot at the end of the season, salmon, when mackerel prices were right down in August. A couple of large salmon might be worth as much as the rest of the catch. We went trotting with mackerel towards the end of the year. First year of our own boat we rowed everywhere and the second year we had a small engine. Working on the quarries, we could afford it. Joey would say, 'If you're doing well, that's not the time to ease up.' These older men were hard but they had lots of wisdoms, showed us how to do everything. When we went out on our own we'd come by Joey's house on the way home and he'd take his share. He'd know exactly what we'd caught. He'd say, 'I'll have those sole you had,' and how he knew we didn't know, 'cos we'd buried them in the bucket, not put them on top. He was watching us with the glass, right up

Uncle Sunny Saunders (postcard from Rab's collection).

(Sunny) Saunders Presentation

The seine boat Sunny was gifted was paraded through the streets of Fortuneswell and the rest of the island, and large crowds threw money into the boat, which Sunny used to buy his nets and gear (postcard from Rab's collection).

the beach. He'd have the glass on us and he knew exactly what we'd caught, 'e'ed keep his eyes on everything from his house.

They used to shoot 'b'launte' up at Chickerell, that is to say, a venture shot. They'd have a net – perhaps not as big and sturdy as ours as the water wasn't so deep. They'd tie on lengths of extra rope to the net and let the ropes out – and a lot of it was by chance. They didn't know if they'd catch much, wouldn't bother to see the shoals coming down on the off-chance. We only shot 'b'stroud', we would see the fish straying black in the water. It was either a big shot for us or we didn't bother. We'd get the slings over the hose and up underneath, two men had to get wet and they had a shot and a half for getting wet, it was dangerous. When the sea come in, the fish would float with the sea. If you got caught, you might have a leg underneath un afore the next sea came in. Half a crew on either side to pull the bottom rope an' pull the slings under the fish, then you would take the two ropes and you'd put the whole crew on to

The crew of the Admiralty trawler (minesweeper) *James Fennell* with Sunny
Saunders, who saved them when their vessel was wrecked in thick fog bound
from Gibraltar to Portsmouth in 1920. Sunny saved the naval ratings by
getting within 30 feet of the vessel and throwing a rope attached to a hawser.
The Captain fell into the sea, and Sunny jumped in and saved him too
(postcard from Rab's collection).

pull the fish up in the slings. Heavy. Still three tonne. If it was too
heavy you'd roll the net back and shovel them out. Used to get wet
of course, and smell a lot. Never swum, can't swim now.

When the weather comes up through the channel you start
with a southwest wind, then it goes westerly and perhaps even
northwesterly, so any wrecks end up this way. There's been cases
of seamen drowned, certain periods of the tide, drowned on boats
washed ashore as wrecks. Instead of staying with the boat for
someone to pass a rope over they'd jumped overboard and couldn't
get to the beach 'cos the sea wouldn't let 'em. It would keep them off.
They'd drown exhausted. Biggish sea rolls up and in over the top to
the first ledge. Six- or eight-foot deep, filters through pebbles and
the rest pours back in volume. What it does, if you look on certain
days in the right conditions, you can see it. That large amount of

sea, when it pours back, it goes under the next sea. It comes out at the back. If you look at the back of the sea, the one just broke, you can see the seas rolling out from the previous sea. Difficult to explain. Once the tide's run out, that volume doesn't come pouring back as the beach is no longer occupied by the sea, it ceases. It's only just after high water with maximum volume of water that it pours underneath. That's why you see rafts of weeds that don't come shore until slack water. The backwash keeps them off. The wind is driving 'em on the beach but it can't come ashore. 'Don't want to bother, boy, they ain't coming ashore yet,' Joey would tell me if I'd said, 'Joey, there's some fine sticks off in the weed.' You'd have to spend a lifetime here to know it all.

The flood runs two and a half hours after high water. The flood is still running at the Bill, that's why on the first of the ebb, the seas get bigger than they do when the flood's down and there's less seas. They ain't so big as when the ebb comes in and when the ebb comes in and there's slacker water the seas rise up. Imagine that volume of water; you might be eighty- or ninety-foot deep and it's all travelling at seven knots. That helps to keep the sea down, so you don't get such a nasty sea when the flood's down as when the ebb's down. On the east side of the island, the ebb is stronger than the flood, and the flood is stronger on the west side than the ebb.

The ebb coming down off the Bill will turn the flood round – does it here too if you look up the beach to where the checkpoint (on the Causeway) is, there's a bump in the beach like this, not so noticeable, then it goes on. That's there because when all the beach is driven westward, as the tide drops and therefore slackens, the pebbles drop out the turbulence of the sea; up to that point they're carried on. The first of the ebb picks up the last of the flood just there. That is why there's more pebbles in that area than anywhere else. If you wasn't a beach hand you wouldn't know this. You get a tide – you've got to have the right weather conditions, mind, for it to show up – and off of that bump in the beach that we're talking about, in the right weather conditions, there's some agitated water, there's a dark patch that can stretch out quarter of a mile or more, what the old fellas used to call 'westgoin', where the ebb tide comes down and meets the flood.

A way of life gone for ever. When I was a boy there was fifty-two boats on this beach between Lods House and the top of Brandy Row. I know this as Uncle Sunny and I often counted them. The fishing was good in those days and although a few men fished on their own, most boats had a two-man crew for potting and netting the long line, one to haul and one to row, some fathers and sons. But mostly mates, so that's a hundred families relying on the fishing to help make ends meet. I loved life on the beach and I got on well with the old men that fished it, well most of them.

Bugger, we've covered some ground but only scratched the surface. It's a lifetime. These things you'd just take for granted, like old recipes, lots of simple procedures they didn't bother to write down as it was obvious at the time. At the time you don't think things will ever change but they do. Who would ever think the mackerel would go, but they have.

7
Chickerell

Sandra Fretwell (b. 1953)

We used to walk across the fields and down to the shed where they kept the gear and nets. There were about half a dozen boats that all rowed across the channel marked out by poles and then they pulled them [trows] up the beach and they also had huts the other side. The crews were all men from Chickerell village. I was still at primary school at the time. They'd catch huge amounts of mackerel, and we ate whatever they caught, so I was brought up on mackerel, lobster, crab, quiddle… We ate mackerel until it came out of our ears, but I still love it. We'd eat it fried or soused in vinegar.

Sundays everyone went over [to the beach], everyone. You see, there wasn't anything else to do. We didn't watch TV and we didn't stay indoors. It was special to us, and a treat to be taken over there. We'd go across on Sundays with all of our extended family; all the uncles (Leonard and Geoffrey Beale) and their families, and the mothers with picnic baskets. Fond memories, all those Sundays with picnics whilst the men fished, and a walk to Moonfleet. That was our stomping ground really, all along the Fleet. It was very much like being in an Enid Blyton adventure, my childhood, the summers were free. Freedom to roam and explore and swim in the shallows and paddle and catch minnows and shrimps, and they used to get us to catch shrimps in nets and buckets from the other side of the pier and then we'd go home for tea across the fields and

Opposite: Marjorie Ireland, née Northover (photo by Pauline Rook).

pick the shrimp for boiling. I was mainly with the other kids from the terrace in the row where we lived. It was a free way of living.

My father, Henry Beale, he was one of the boat co-owners in charge of his crew, but they all used to love going over to beach. He'd go over on his own, row over there and sit on the beach. It was his life and he kept going over until he died. He was a real countryman, always out and about doing something. He worked at the brickworks where they were digging the clay, making and firing the bricks, plus he had an allotment, was a beater for the Abbotsbury estate sometimes, looked after the fishing crew and boats and helped with the ledgers and accounts. But he'd row over and sit on the beach – 'just to look see if it's still there,' he'd say. He loved beach.

It was fascinating to watch [the seining], even as a young girl. Sometimes it was my job to keep the boat, keep it steady in the tide, keep the fish down, but what I really remember very strongly is the rhythm of the men working – seeing the crews in two lines on the arms of the net to land the catch whilst I was keeping the boat. There were several men on each side opposite each other and what I really remember very strongly is the image of how they'd all dig their heels into the pebbles to take the strain; they dug their heels in, all leaning back. It was so heavy, the net. Leaning back then they'd get into a sort of swinging rhythm. Swinging one arm down all together, dropping that arm, heaving up the line on their shoulders on the shout of 'pull', which my father sometimes shouted, and then it was: swing arm back drop heave up swing arm back drop heave up, on the shout. Just like that. All in time. They had to keep in rhythm to pull it in, slow and steady, really tough work. It was a different kind of mindset, it was such hard work. No one ever sat around the house.

Dennis Harman (b. 1952)

There used to be two piers at Chickerell Hive built opposite each other, landing stages with lights on posts, either side of the channel in the water, used during the war to fool the enemy into believing that the Fleet was a runway in the dark. There was a generator in one of the huts for the lights. There was a large painted arrow on the ground pointing towards the Fleet which was lit up. There isn't much left of the piers now, but you can still see the posts on the Fleet side.

We'd go down early when I was working, and after we had caught the fish and we were in the process of boxing them up, we would be on our knees early morning and someone would look up and see the sun starting to appear over the top of the beach. They'd say: 'Aye up, Lawrence is up.' I'm pretty sure the fish buyer's name was Lawrence. Maybe it was said because it was as if he was peeping over the beach to see if we had caught anything.

There were plenty of days it was raining hard – there were huts men could retreat to but mostly we carried on in the rain. Although the men would be getting wetter they'd still be making a joke of the situation. That's why you couldn't do it just for the money; sometimes there were no fish. It was good fun and good friends with my dad's crew, a way of life. You'd never come home disappointed if you didn't catch. There's been a few times crossing the Fleet I could tell you about... Edward Carter once got caught in fog in a trow loaded with fish for pick-up. In the fog he turned around and rowed straight back to the Chesil with the fish. Same happened to me once. You can find your way in the dark with years of experience but the fog can be disorienting, and you'd think it would be easy to cross the Fleet. I've known people that've swum in the Fleet. Philip Gollop swam the Channel and his coach had him in the Narrows to train against the tide, but the water is generally much shallower now than it used to be.

Edward Marshallsay (b. 1960)

I grew up fishing. I know the beach as much as anybody, but it very much depends on what part you're on. At Moonfleet, where I was, it's secluded, you're on your own basically. Less people have access to get across so you have to imagine the fishing crews who get across they'd be over there on their own most times.

Me Dad [David] and me grandad [Albert 'Toby' Marshallsay], they'd always fished. You went automatically. I'd fished all the time through school. I could earn money on the beach. I had motorbikes, brand-new. It's a job to explain. When I was a child it was an evening crew 'cos all the men were at work in the daytime, but as the years went by they formed a daytime and evening crew as the guys retired, so I left school at the right time and walked into it. We had daytime and mostly evening crews and then high days and holidays... I remember Whit week was a week a lot of men had off, took time off and spent it over fishing together. I could name the hands now – Chummy, Boyce, Tom Collins, Ed Carter, and Johnny Randall sometimes, I was there... Tony Beale when he wasn't on duty – he was a policeman.

It was just our way of life, it was really. Your father went because he wanted to earn a shilling, you went with him to be part of it. All working with Chummy the whole time. You fish tides, a young flood or slack of the ebb, spec shooting, then later in the year shoaling fish as they strayed, that was a short shot around them.

It was hard work, everything done by hand, although we had a tractor for the ship end and a capstan. It was a long way off the beach whilst you were pulling it [the net] in. You could see the circular corks. It was way off the beach, and when the fish are alive, they're swimming so it's nothing whilst you're pulling in. When you got in nearer the shore, the fish are on the beach and nearer the ground; that's when you have to use the tractor for the load or cut and dip. At the end of the seine was what they called the 'hose'. If you had a lot of fish it would be full up and there was no way a tractor would pull it up. You anchored the net with the tractor, cut the net and shovelled the fish out and carried up onto the beach. Depends on how many you had. Sometimes they'd come with a hessian sack and wet it down for the fish with another sheet to cover the fish netted down. Years ago they were picked up and put in the six-stone baskets when I was a child, and the men would carry them up over the beach and carried over in wooden boxes. In recent times we had the tractor, stacked on the tractor... loaded into trows.

They were stacked up at Fleet House. If it was dry they were stacked on the shore so the lorry could get down over the bank, but if it was wet you had to carry them up over the bank so the lorry didn't have to come down over. Greenslades turned up and picked them up – Frank Greenslade, Ken Greenslade, Lawrence Greenslade. Once it started, they knew as well as we did when we'd fish. The trow will take one hundred stone if it's stacked right. I used to keep a tally for Chum. We were then taking fish from Fiddler's Lake up to Fleet House and the lorry would come across the field, picked the fish up there. The old boat house that's there, the roof tiles, red-clay tiles, I used to scribe on bits of tile like how many boxes of large mackerel, medium mackerel, small mackerel, etc etc, and I'd drop it off at his house which was over the road on the way back, and then he wrote that down and sorted the money out accordingly, like.

Park Wall were one of the highest catchers on the beach. There were some characters. Charl Randall, incredible character. Generally nice guy, not a lot younger than Chummy. Tom Collins [whom Dennis also remembers, as 'a strong man, always with a tin of snuff over on the beach.'] Boyce, another character. Walley Randall. We looked up to these men, me and me brother.

The crews were very secretive. Even to the point that if you come ashore with the net, and you could tell if you knew what we were doing, you could tell when the net was twenty to thirty yards off the shore. You knew – I mean you couldn't see what was in it but you could tell if there was any amount of fish. What used to happen quite frequently was the other crews that be down the beach would be watching you with binoculars, no doubt at all, so it was like everybody get down there and make out that we've got a load of fish when we haven't. You'd have half a dozen blokes down there pretending. That was the trick, trick the other people you knew were watching you with binoculars, and they did the same, that's what used to happen, trick them into putting their net out again. What the hell point of it was I'm not sure. I wasn't the instigator of all that! I do recollect stones being thrown at some point, I do recollect that.

I enjoyed it. When a wave came in over the boat it was happy days, like. Not sure so much now. You got wet, there's no ifs or buts about it. When they used to sling them, that was wet. Far too many fish to pull out, they used to sling them with a heavy-duty small net they'd put around the fish in the hose so they could handle it. Job to explain it. I've lost count of times when there was that many fish you just can't do nothing with it. Bundle is an 'out knife and cut job,' the old men would say. We've all seen this, same amount of times whoever you talk to. When you had a big catch and there was a sea running with waves breaking over whilst you were dipping the fish, it could get a bit heated, a lot of language flying around like, lots of swearing.

I was in a boat one Sunday afternoon. Chummy chucked the seine out. Charl Randall was on one after oar and Edward Carter was on the other after oar and me and me father were on both bow oars. We shot the seine out and were coming ashore with the ship end. Now coming shore, sometimes you haul the boat out when you come ashore, and sometimes someone kept it. We were going to haul the boat out, backing to the shore, backing onto the shore, and we mistimed it. Boat turned over, bit of a mess all over the place.

Eventually got out of trouble and that was Chummy Northover's brain got us out of trouble. We pulled the net ashore – I don't remember there was much fish – and then we were quarter of a mile down the beach with the tide, the boat had to be retrieved. My old man, Charl Randall and Chummy went to get the boat but they wouldn't let me go, it were real nasty. Chummy was renowned for shooting in ridiculous seas at times. On the other hand, he was very good at it… Looking back on it, it's easy to panic at the time. Looking back, common sense played a large part to it. Believe it or not, you got a high out of it, I did anyway.

Do we miss it? Depends who you talk to. I come from Chickerell, and there's several people that I can still talk to and they'd understand. It's not a different language, but I can say things and they'd know what I was on about. Them days are all gone but there's still a few of us about.

8

Langton Herring

Gail McGarva with Ian Reeder (b. 1948) and Ken Gowans (b. 1928)

Gail: *What are your first memories of the lerret and seine fishing?*

Ken: I started at sixteen from Chickerell. At the weekend you had seventeen or eighteen hands with Les Hinton, 'Mac' McCadden, Ted Harman. The boat was *Jubilee*. They had a syndicate, Chappie Beale and Les. It was somewhere to go, something to do. I loved fishing.

Ian: I come fishing up here all the time. There was a lerret up here then when I was fifteen, *Girl Pat*. Uncle Joe Frampton had it. Uncle Joe, he wasn't very good at looking after boats. His idea of boat maintenance was chucking a bucket of tar on and push it about with the sweeping brush… then the *Vera* come up. She was up Abbotsbury at the time. They say they'd gotten him off Harold Richards. Looked alright, the shape was there, he looked alright, so we give fifty quid for him… then pushed him off the back wall and he sunk. Then we bailed him out and he sunk, we bailed him out and he sunk. I could see he was alright really… In the winter we took him back to Chickerell.

Ken: Pulled it all to pieces and then we done him up. We done everything on him. All the new ribs, seats, knees, gunwales and some new planks. Worked all the way round. Took him down the shore in the summer, pushed him afloat and away he went. No

Opposite: Ken Gowans at Langton Beach (photo by Pauline Rook).

bother at all and we had him for years. Never touched him after that, varnished him all up and he looked a picture. An absolute picture, never touched him after, forty years. Brilliant after that. It was worth doing.

And Vera *was built in 1923?*

Ian: 1923 he was built, by Wills and Carter for Tom Randall, made the same year his daughter Vera was born. All the boats I know all built around that time. She (Vera Randall) passed away, buried about three weeks ago… Shame really, 'cos she'd have been good to talk to, she would.*

Can you describe the process of the fishing at this location to me?

Ken: We always had a high heart; we'd caught half of them before we ever got here Sunday mornings. Sometimes they'd stray. I used to stay on the beach. Worked the line. You've got a tide running. Ebb or flowing, you know. And you have to keep ahead of that tide. You can't have it straight out in front of you, otherwise you're in trouble. You've gotta sort of go down there and keep it on an angle all the time. They've got a job to keep theirs, 'cos they've got to come on all the time, you know, with the winch.

Ian: As long as you keep in front of the tide, look. Holding the ship end, you're fighting against the tide all the time… especially when you used to back it up, you know. I mean that was hard work backing up. I mean, well, we always used to do it… We never had no leaky boats, dangerous having a leak. It's coming shore with the rollers. When you come ashore, if it's nasty, you've got to keep the boat straight. Keep the boat straight and it's no bother. If there's a lot of water in it, you can't keep straight. If he

* We think that Vera, the daughter, may also have been named for the famous wreck of a steamer off Langton. The remains of the vessel remained for some time; such physical obstacles to seine fishing were known as 'fastenings'. The wreck was famous for the courage of the volunteer Auxiliary Coastguards who saved all twenty-seven crew by rocket apparatus. Many of the volunteers involved in the rescue were Langton fishermen.

Vera, one of the last lerrets launching (photo by Keith Pritchard).

goes round you've just, you've had it… You only want two inches of water under a lerret and he's gone, on that one we got, anyway. And when you're pushing him afloat, I mean you gotta be careful 'cos he's gone and you're left in the guts of the sea, if you don't be careful. He is, he's that good.

Who would be on the boat ashore?

Ian: The crew would be on the boat, and the bloke who was chucking the seine would call for the push. We had some good hands. They'd been doing it all their lives. Tom Randall, Joseph Frampton, best bloke on the beach you'd ever seen – pushing afloat or getting shore, we used to go out when it was nasty.

What about the mackerel?

Ken: You know you got 'em when you see what we call a 'rudd'. Cut 'em up on the dip net running up and down with the pots. Some good times. I still love it, I'd have it over again.

A good sense of feeling between you all?

Ian: Yeh, difficult to explain.

But you were saying earlier, about when someone goes down the beach it's like something else comes over them, another part of their character.

Ian: It's the salt air I reckon. I don't know, it's funny.

Ken: Are they there or aren't they there?

Ian: Especially when mackerel are straying, lot of fish. Usually a wet job.

Ken: I used to really enjoy it, sort of lived for it.

Ian: As long as you got a good crew. We always had a good crew. I mean it's potentially dangerous, you know. When it's nasty it is, but I mean we always had a good crew, people around you all the time who knew what they were doing, you know. I mean, it can be. Pushing you afloat's the most dangerous. You know, pushing a boat afloat is quite a responsible job, you know... Tom Randall, he was a bloody lion, son of the man who owned *The Vera*, look. If it's pebbles you're fine, you'll go, but I mean if it's gritty the boat will come down, hit the grit and he'll stop dead. I seen Thomas on there and you'll see the sides of the boat start going out as he's pushing on that stern post. The boat was either going to split in two or he was going to float, I tell you...

Ken: Yeh, it's true. He was a powerful bloke. He used to work in the brickyard then.

Ian: Well, we all did. Hell of a nice bloke. We had so many good people on the crew. That's what you got to have. But you didn't want to upset him, you didn't want to upset him at all.

What's the process once you have the fish, cross the Fleet?

Ken: I saw poor old Donald Peach and he picked the wrong trow, one what leaked. He's only halfway across with a hundred stone of mackerel and he sunk. Donald never swore either, did he?

I bet those trows were full to the brim, weren't they?

Ken: Used to put them straight into the trow once, pots on your back that was hard work.

Ian: Longest carry on the beach up here. Sore back when you finished. We used to have terns dive-bombing us, you know, at nesting time.

Ken: There were fair big crews on that beach, mind, a fair few, couple at Portland. You had Ted Ruffle at Wyke – he didn't have it for long. You had Harold Richards at Wyke, you had Chappie and all them at Chickerell Hive. Sammy Randall's father at Chickerell. You had Chummy at Park Wall, George Frampton, you had people what lived here, you had Jim Taylor, what was called the 'co-ops' fishing from Langton. You had Aish Huddy at Abbotsbury. He used to come Chickerell early part of the year. He had boats all the way down to West Bay.

Ian: Another one born and bred to it, family.

Ken: He learned me something. We was down west side of Cogden and there's rocks west side of Cogden and mackerel was straying and they would not come off the rocks. He was there and he picked up some rocks, small pebbles and kept flicking them like that, drove 'em off the rocks, and he had 'em. Knew all the tricks. Had a lovely crew, with Betty in the stern and Lizzie. Girls used to work as hard as any of them. He was a good bloke to be with, actually. Yeah… All gone now though. End of an era.

That's why we're here before it's lost forever. What do you think changed?

Ian: Youngsters don't seem to want to take it on now. They went to beach 'cos they had to, start with, that was the thing. They needed the money in those days. I mean, you go back to the 1920s, look, there wasn't no social. You couldn't go and draw any money, look. I mean everybody went to beach.

Ken: We all went to beach night-time, everybody. They used to line up the Langton crew, line 'em up, out the road up there. 'I'll 'ave you, I'll 'ave you…' Like that. And that was for the season that was.*

---

* There was an article in *Chesil Magazine*, August 1980, by Mr C. Chipps talking about the fishing at Langton Herring in his grandfather's era. He wrote: '… when the wind was making the sea rough and dirty, the men decided that they couldn't fish although it was fine and warm inshore. Some was along the road, they all sat down to rest, a passer-by counted them, there were eighty-four men.'

Ian: Have you seen the fishing rules? Even had bit of sick pay. All sorts. People don't understand they lived off fishing. There wasn't nothing else to eat. You had mackerel in the summer and you salted 'em and you had mackerel in the winter, look. Devoted to it. They needed the money in them days, see? Nowadays they don't.

A way of life…

Ian: You grew into a way of life.

Ken: You'd light the fire for breakfast, put the old bucket of salt water on, a little mackerel, take the scum off once, let it boil again, take the scum off again, then tip 'em out. They were absolutely beautiful. Bread and butter, that's all it was.

Ian: Always had the kettle on the go, somebody was always boiling the kettle.

Ken: From four o'clock in the morning you might be home by four o' clock in the afternoon if you're lucky.

A real physical endeavour…

Ken: We went spratting in winter at West Bay. That was worse mind, you really felt it then. Fifteen hundred stone catch 'em in one shot. Lorry used to line up. Aish Huddy was down there, even a crew from Weymouth down there, Bert Legg and Henry Donne down there. That was later on. Used to get down there around two o'clock in the morning. Wait for daylight. Aish was always there already waiting, always had the first throw, would wait for them to come off the rocks and that was it.

Did you make the nets for Vera?

Richard (Andrews) did most of the nets… Joseph Frampton could do it with his eyes shut.

Where did you put Vera in winter?

Ian: Everything was pulled up here for working on the boats over winter from October or whenever the season finished. Ideal pulled up here. You don't feel the wind in here, it seems to bounce off the top of you. The square-backs and lerret, trow. Everything came up. We never left anything down there in the winter.

Ken: Yeh, good times, when we had both the boats, we worked both of them one time.

But the difference in the performance of them with the square-stern and the lerret... very very different.

Ken: Yeh, they're rubbish square-sterns.

Ian: The lerret was the ideal boat for this beach, especially in the sea, meant for it, bob about, go anywhere. No bother at all in the lerret... you could go anywhere in a lerret, I reckon. We've caught some fish and we sometimes ain't caught some fish. Ain't catching if they ain't there.

Ken: Yeh, there was always that element of doubt, you know. Are you going to get something? We used to say to one another coming up in the car, you know: 'What do you reckon we'll have tonight?' 'Ohhh, we'll have a few tonight,' and finish up with nothing. We've had thousand stone or more, but the crews got smaller, we finished with seven hands, but we had the tractor then for the ship end on the shoulder.

Ian: Took a bit of getting used to. Lot of weight going back and forward....nylon net made a difference too. Cotton used to get wet and heavy. They used to make seine every year. Saved a lot of work nylon did.

Ken: You got to love fishing. My wife was a beach widow she was. We had three children and she didn't see me half the time.

End of an era...

Ian: You won't see no more.

9
Abbotsbury

Pat Donnelly (b. 1934)

In 1947 we moved from South London, ow, a bitter winter it was. We lived in the old coastguard cottages. My mother ran a guest house and had to provide three cooked meals a day and cope with rationing and all the postwar problems... I finished school and worked on the Ilchester Estates, then I went into the army for three years, then I worked on putting the mains water in at Abbotsbury and Portesham. You're ten miles from the nearest town in any direction from Abbotsbury. There wasn't much work around then and I think my mother went and talked to Ash. It was a job you know.

Ash had a hut on the beach, a narrow wooden building with a fire in one corner, and odd chairs either side, and a small annex on the end of it, and on the end of that was a toilet for the ladies. You'd all pile in the hut and they had a blackened kettle that went on the fire... there was nothing hanging up because there was no need for anything, no spare net, you know, maybe coats. We'd perhaps have a shot and then they'd say it was time for breakfast and I'd pop home and I might go to bed if they said we weren't going to have another shot until after lunch.

It was hard physical work, with only five of us and only two really who'd carry the fish up and over the beach with a basket on your back, and that was me and Ashley [Arnold]. Bushel baskets – they

Opposite: Betty Arnold selling fish at the top of Abbotsbury beach, next to the hut (courtesy of Alan Arnold).

had a rope off that you hold over your shoulder and you'd carry it to the fish buyer and his lorry; he'd weigh them into boxes. You did what you were told, and you were cursed if you did anything wrong. When I was fishing the skin on my hands was a quarter of an inch thick from pulling on ropes and oars. If you'd got mackerel straying you'd see the oars bend when you were pulling on them.

The copse of the oar was what you pulled the boat over, depends on where the boat was. In the morning the seines were laid out across the beach to dry and boat pulled right up, and you'd have to push it down. We'd only grease them [oars] if Ash had been into town to Harry Balem the butcher in Weymouth. You had to be careful when you have a boat on copse-greased oars as it goes down rather rapidly. We always had a lucky stone in the boat... I gave one to the cancer consultant in Poole recently...

It was just turn up [everyday] and join in with the other four, Ash, Ashley, Lizzie and Betty, the full-time crew. It was a team, it had to be otherwise it wouldn't work, if literally you didn't pull your weight... we all muddled along together. We had a dog in the crew called Spot. Other Estate workers and members of the Arnold family came down weekends and evenings. Ash was the skipper and he decided everything, anything from four o'clock in the morning onwards depending on the time of year.

You'd get down to the boat and usually Ash was on the ship end on the beach, Ashley and I would row round with Lizzy throwing the seine, Bet would probably be with Ash, we'd come round, pull the boat out and it's just a question of hauling the seine. You come down to the sea, put the rope onto your shoulder, walk up across to reach the rudge and go back down, a rotating chain hauling the seine in as you take the strain. As you haul the seine in, the tide is taking you along the beach as well. You could see all the lines of footsteps coming across the beach. When we rowed out to 'the ledge' with hand lines, it was further out. They knew the ledge through marks but I didn't know the marks. When we got to the ledge we dropped a kellick overboard, a bag of shingle, like an anchor, but would not get caught up in the rocks.

There wasn't much banter; practical things like 'plugs not in', you know, or you'd watch the holes in the net as they go over, and say, 'Hang on Lizzy, they're not tied'… and we'd come in again and she'd pull in the bunt and tie the holes up.

Saturday is the rest day for a fishing crew. Ashley and me used go into town to the pictures and have a drink and catch the bus back in the evening. Ash Huddy didn't drink. He was wiry, strong, had a wealth of knowledge about fishing and seines, some self-taught, some from the old fishermen at Wyke where he grew up. He never married, neither did Lizzie or Ashley. He never went out of an evening, went to the workshop where he kept the nets and stores. They all lived together in that house, the Arnolds, and there'd been nine of them growing up there, not sure what the living arrangements were. He came during or after the war. There's a story that Ash was one of those who'd been kept behind and meant to form an underground army if we were invaded, trained in espionage, blowing things up… it wouldn't surprise me at all if it were true. He later had a motorboat in Weymouth harbour and a lerret, *Queen Mary*, and two others, and he had one other boat at Bexington with the Puncknowle crew, the Millers.

I remember waking up one morning and we'd been fishing and it was alright, I went home and I'd gone to bed and I woke up and thought bloody hell, and there was a big swell come in from nowhere, so I shot into the village and called hands 'cos the boat was at Chickerell and luckily we got there because if the sea had come and covered the net it would've been hell's own job to get it out from under the pebbles. The sea hadn't come up to it but it came from nowhere. Normally you didn't hear the sea, you see, like living near a busy road and you don't hear the cars, but the groundswell is different; it's a 'boom' sort of noise and then you hear all the beach being dragged out, dragged back.

Lizzy and Betty Arnold hauling in the seine, Abbotsbury beach.

Then I remember there was a strip of field between Ash's hut and the old coastguards' and they used to say that in the Depression, itinerant workers used to camp there and see if they could get any money in the shot [of the seine]. It was known as *Shit and Can*. The 'can' part might refer to a local word for the freshwater stream running alongside the field; the name described the basic facilities.

There was another thing I heard. The swanherd Fred Lexster used to tell us about a time the press gangs came to Abbotsbury back in the day. Two fishermen ran and hid, one up in Jubilee woods and the other wore his wife's bedclothes and hid in the bed under the covers.

Winters we went logging, which started after Christmas, and we also cut the reed beds for the thatch for the Estate. They had their own thatcher then, Freddie Burden. One year, herring appeared in December and Ashley and I would go out with one end of the drift net and with Ash and the others ashore. We would paddle along to keep the net at right angles to the shore. Bitter cold, it was, and dark when we went afloat. When we saw the smoke from Freddie Burden's cottage, we knew it was time to land. Herrings squeak, did you know that... they squeak like mice when you land them, now you don't expect that.

We went to West Bay for the sprats one year, our biggest catch was I think fourteen tonnes, but we hauled them up the beach and the drag wore the nets, we lost a lot of fish because of that... Most I ever earned was £60 in one week but it was usually £10 a week or so and you had to pay a stamp. Then I got married and you couldn't rely on it, you see, for a regular living. Ashley and Lizzie finished up making nets and camouflage for the net-makers in Bridport. It's a long time ago, I'm one of the last, you see.

Pete Stevens (b. 1951)

We used to come down to Chickerell in the spring of the year sometimes, as the water didn't clear so well up our way as it's not so deep. Sometimes you'd hear they'd caught mackerel down Chickerell, so we'd have trows to get across and put a boat and seine down in the spring of the year. All the men came together and talked and they were watching. A lot of people wouldn't tell you how many they'd had, but the part-timers drank in the pubs together and bragged sometimes. There was a lot of people fishing when I first started. We counted up around twenty sometimes on the crews. Sometimes we'd have three boats and seines if there was mackerel straying and we'd break up into three boats.

My father, Bill Stevens, was a part-time fisherman, then there was the Ropers, me great-uncle was a Roper, come with us in the end. There were a lot of fishermen in the family going back, not sure how far they went back, there was always someone in the Arnolds fishing. Shep Arnold was me grandfather, Ashley [Arnold] was me uncle, Lizzie and Betty [Arnold] were aunties. They all went fishing full-time from when the war was on with Huddy. Not sure how he came to be in Abbotsbury; trouble is there's no one to tell you now.

I sat out in the boat at six or seven, keeping the boat, where you go along with the tide and the boat will be there when you come ashore. It's only a matter of floating along when it's dead-smooth for the youngsters, then if it's rough you have to tie the heaving line on the bunt cork. When you pull the seine out round, you keep along with the tide in front of the seine. You want a good person on the long end to keep in front and help you pull ashore; at the ship end they had the longer part to pull in. Sometimes, if we thought the fish were swimming high, you'd go over on the first quarter above the net to make sure the fish come down into the net. The person keeping the boat would help to keep the fish down.

I wanted to seine, it was exciting really. I wish you could see it. There must be so many films of us in rough seas, there were so many holidaymakers with cine cameras, loads of them, never seen any film. People won't believe how rough a sea we used to go in. I've been off and we've got out to the end of the net and had to wait to get a smooth to turn to come in. Fish would always come in generally before a blow, and the water would be clear then but after a blow it would be stirred up, so they'd be off further.

Have you ever seen the mackerel in rough seas when they swim up through the sea? When they stray all the water splashes, but when it's rough and they're coming right in swimming in the guts of the sea, they're swimming up through the water, you just see the backs of them, greeny-blue, you just see them like darts through clear water.

Years ago then at Chickerell when we saw little terns we knew to have a go. They didn't like us down there and we didn't like it when they came up our way.

Abbotsbury crew dipping out mackerel (great-uncle Fred Roper second from left).

'Cos of the 'fastenings' [fixed obstacles in the water], as they call it, where a plane come down, you could only shoot the net up so far, but you had to get up to catch the tide down to where you wanted to land, and if there was someone else there you had to wait. What we done is had two boats and seines out, got one in, they had one, then we'd do another one in between.

We had one lerret, *Queen Mary*, for night-time, then we had *Kingfisher* and *Sprat* – those were both square-sterns – and then Ash had *Chesil Queen* built but it wasn't as good. For some reason he wouldn't be a good go for really rough seas, not the best anyway, never had the lift in the middle. *Queen Mary* was roughest I've been out in.

'Chickllers', as we used to call them, used to come up and say, you could have all our boys for your one boy, and that was me. I've always looked at what people do and then get on and do it rather than stand back. I was always in the boat, never chucked the seine though.

Have you ever seen a groundswell down there, really? You can hear it from here, hear it growling down there and it won't always be when the wind's blowing. They had a wind out in the Atlantic and it comes in after and that's what people don't realise is the worst time, because the sea is rolling a long distance and that's when you get an undertow. Sometimes January or February it'll drag all the beach off. Not all of it, but a fair bit of the beach all along, and people have been there and picked up gold coins and all that before. You can hear it and we always used to go down and we'd go and get the lead weights left by the anglers. You could hear it at Abbotsbury sometimes. Fish was even straying once and we shot stupidly 'cos there was so many and we lost all of the net 'cos of the drag when it's coming through, couldn't hold it. There was some fisherman up the road on a pleasure boat hooking fish that went ashore to pick someone up and they turned the boat over, two were drowned. I must have been fifteen then. They come in sideways and the swell smashed the boat like it was cardboard. Such a long drag, and if there's a swell you wouldn't have got in. You can come ashore on a sea but you have to wait for the moment and keep on top of the wave, not too quick, a lot of people wouldn't know how to manage it.

We tipped the boat once. Ash and me put the boat out which was normal, he was good at judging the waves, but our uncle Ashley went off outside the breakers and a little wave flipped him over and the boat come straight in, and Ash always said to me after, 'I'm glad you was as strong as you was', what with the suction and with the breakers breaking over us and someone underneath the boat, and we lifted it and just got a bit of air in and he crawled out. It was just us three there on beach at the time. He was getting old then, Ashley. Ash always said if it'd been anyone else we mightn't have got him out.

Abbotsbury crew trainees, left to right: Jimmy Pitman, Alan Arnold and Fred Langford (courtesy of Alan Arnold).

I fished six or seven years, but I was bunking off school before that. My uncle would say: 'The bait's in, be here tomorrow.' By the time I left school I had more money than I've ever had. I'd saved about seven hundred pounds… When I think about it now… Back then you spent it.

The best year ever was with the night-time crewing. We'd have reached twelve hundred stone each week for six weeks. One Sunday we caught over a thousand stone. That was when I was only a boy. We seen 'a trip' of mackerel, as we used to call it, and we had two crews out and one of the crews went up just under Greenbanks where they start. I walked up the beach and there's mackerels going down, so I waved them in and this is what come in the lawn end and we had three hundred stone and they had six or seven hundred stone in the net up the beach.

People don't realise how tiring it was. My gran used to come round and make sure I was up 'cos if they came round in the lorry and you wasn't ready they wouldn't wait. They all worked hard, tired, it was a hard life in them days. My father was grumpy as well, but he'd come back from the war and never talked about it. He worked six days a week on the lorry, then came fishing night-times and Sundays; that was one of the main days. Before I went to school I used to go with Ash to feed the cats he kept at the hut for the rats. We used to sleep down at the hut as schoolboys. Ash was alright. He had a boat up at Weymouth and every Saturday he'd go and watch the football in Weymouth at the Rec. He played football for Weymouth when he was younger, nearly trialled for Leicester, but there was more money in fishing back then.

For the seining, you work the tides. You'd have probably a couple of hours fishing and then you'd have to get rid of the fish if you caught any. First of all you had to carry them up, then we had a sled made to pull them up to the lorry on a track and pulley. Ray Laver was our buyer from Puncknowle. Sometimes be five or six shots, and if you hadn't had anything sometimes it'd be more, and we tried out every way. Mainly on the flood tides you caught the fish but sometimes you'd shoot with the tide the other way, ebb tide, and come with the tide. For spotting fish, they used to say best uncle was Dave Arnold. Lizzie done the breakfast whilst we were getting the fish up. Sometimes we cooked mackerel in the bucket with water from the sea. Then we'd sleep a while or go out and lie on the beach, under the boats out of the sun. We did well, even on a Sunday we could sell a lot of fish to visitors off the beach. They all came down to buy mackerel, crowds of people watching us. Sometimes it got messy when we were putting the sling on to save the drag on the net. You'd get wet up to your neck or put your head under. Some of them didn't want to get wet, fish scales everywhere. I never wore wellies to beach in my life.

It was hard work but I loved it when it was rough. I was happy doing it but in the end you couldn't sell the fish, couldn't get enough money for them. In the end my mates were on more money... I was about twenty-three when I finished but still came back to fish sometimes. You had to love it really. Nowadays people wouldn't know what to do with a mackerel most of them. Now they're all gone.

Alan Arnold (b. 1957)

I was born on the Fleet at Clouds Hill, my stepfather Dick Dalley was the swanherd and this was the house we lived in, been on the Fleet all my life. We were there until I was fifteen and the generator shed caught fire and we moved into the village; shame really. They knocked it down in the end, Clouds Hill. Dick fished for the Langton crew and then with the Huddys when he met my mother.

Fished all my life. Ash came up to Abbotsbury from Wyke and I don't know how the crew was formed but the Arnolds went with the Huddys and Ash lived with them. His father may have come up here first with his brothers. Used to say he never had any shoes on his feet until sixteen. He was an incredible man; stern, mind. Gained respect from everybody. I was brought up with him.

I used to jump off the school bus from Weymouth and wait for Uncle Dave or Bob Limb to turn up after work and get a lift down to beach and fish into the night, like, every night, soon as I was old enough. All my summer holidays, every single day on that beach and earning a few quid. We were still in our heyday then. I left school fifteen and took it up full-time, the year Ash Huddy died of lung cancer. We went to beach without him. Ashley and Lizzie took over the business.

Some things had altered by then, like the way you transported the fish up the beach. You could catch five hundred stone of mackerel, right, and you got twelve to fourteen hands; those pots hold four-and-a-half stone so every time ten people go up that's forty-five stone shifted. You'd have a massive catch of fish on the beach and some people that're sorting these into medium, large and small pots, then the other people that could carry would carry them to get boxed into wooden tomato boxes and weighed at the top of the beach. It didn't take many trips with the hands they had, shifted faster than you might think.

We had fourteen hands at times. In the evenings you'd get the night crew turned up, five or six more hands, for a couple more shots. Then you might only get thirty stone a shot. You see a shot is like this, the lawn end off… the fish are coming in with the tide but the nets not moving as fast as the tide but the fish are. Fish are always swimming to the west in the spring of the year and beyond so we're always shooting towards the west. As you bring the net in the fish come up against this arm and go off, and the fish always head off the deep water so the half-moon net and the tide forces them back in again, doing a curl until you close them off. The whole shot takes twenty minutes; whatever you catch is what's coming along in that twenty minutes. Sometimes you can have five hundred stone in that twenty minutes. The bay is solid with fish then when it's like that, which I've seen many times. Some years you'll be lucky if you get a hundred stone all year and yet you'll have to keep shooting for them through the tide and make your numbers up. It's nice when you can have one shot, two hundred and fifty stone and go, but sometimes you have to work for them, it varies on the tides. You have to learn the tides, it's quite complex.

Like, if you go to Chickerell the fishing is different to the fishing at Abbotsbury. Certain tides down there you can't catch fish where you can at Abbotsbury. If you go to Chickerell, the best shot to have down there is when the slack of the ebb is going towards Bridport when it's just stopping. If they shoot then, they'll have a bundle. Up Abbotsbury, that rarely happens. The ebb tide at

Ash Huddy looking out for mackerel.

Abbotsbury ramps on a bit more because of the shape of the beach; the further you go to Portland the tide is coming across more but up Abbotsbury it's running full on. You got to wait for the tide to turn and then you have what they call a 'fore flood' – that's the very trickle of the flood. The fore flood, before high water. So if you had fifty or sixty stone on the ebb, on the fore flood you might have hundred and fifty or two hundred stone. Up Abbotsbury the fore flood was our favourite shot.

Depending on if it's neap or spring tides, usually the fish drop off as you get to high water. You don't catch as many as it gets to high water… the first two or three days of the lift up is always a good time, the tide's not too strong, going from neaps to springs, the first couple of days when he starts lifting from the bottom up, that's favourite. The neap tides favour Abbotsbury rather than Chickerell; you could fish the neaps at Chickerell and have nothing and up at Abbotsbury you could have bundles.

They used to start their fishing in April down at Chickerell. It was the equivalent of ten to one; ten stone at Abbotsbury you could have a hundred at Chickerell then. When it gets to May, you go to Abbotsbury, all the Chickerell crews came up to Abbotsbury in May and we'd have to compete with all of those crews – Dave Bartlett's crew, 'Mac' McCadden's crew and all those. Three crews all on the beach lining up to fish the same bit of ground. They stayed right through, spent the rest of the summer up at Abbotsbury sometimes.

I know from fishing here years with my uncle, you can go six weeks some years without catching a mackerel, you know, it's a hard life.

There was some rivalry between crews but no animosity. There'd be three boats lined up with other crews, all waiting for a tide. Uncle Dave used to walk the track and if he saw a shoal of mackerel coming along that we couldn't see from half a mile or a mile away, he would go 'halfway to Bexington', as we'd say, and you'd all keep your eye on him, and if he walked down over the beach you'd know he'd seen fish. He wouldn't wave. You'd have to gingerly get up and all go and get around your boat, push your boat in and paddle on up through as if nothing had happened and then once you'd got past the others then you started rowing so you got up in front of the fish before anyone else to shoot the net, because it was your living. If someone else saw the fish they'd be in as well; it'd be a race to see who'd get to the fish first. Depend on the boat then and your crew and how you can row, how quick you can get to the shoal coming down to the beach. We used to travel to them. If you got one shot all week, that's your week's money, see what I mean? Whoever got there first got the fish.

When I left school at fifteen I knew exactly what I wanted to do. I got offered a job as a farm labourer at £7 a week, but I could go down the beach and earn £30 a week. Bear in mind we were up half past three in the morning and working all the hours god sends, but when the fish was in, we earned good money. You earned £50 in a week sometimes, a lot of money. We shifted some fish for that, mind – two thousand stone of mackerel a week. If you had a good May and June that was your season sorted really. You might be 'fine weather no fish' June and July. If it was good weather for weeks then we loaded the lorry up and went to Seatown for small shoals, chasing whitebait up the beach. You didn't sit and do nothing, you carried on fishing. At the end of the year the Huddy crew went up Preston Beach Road in Weymouth. Then sprat fishing; that'd all finished by the time I was fishing. In one week they caught twenty-two thousand stone on the West Bay pier, long before.

The big problem with the fishing was we couldn't sell the fish like we used to. Once upon a time at the end of the war the demand for the fish was insatiable, with the government subsidy in the early fifties, and they earned a fortune from the sprats then. That meant you could catch as much as you liked and declare what you caught and got a shilling a stone subsidy, a fortune in them days. You could sell everything you could catch, but I suppose people ate more fish.

Don't think you can tell if it'll be a good or bad year for fishing. Last week of April then first weeks of May are sometimes not much good but towards middle of May that's when the fish used to arrive and you could start seriously having bundles of fish. April, May it can be smooth as a pond and clear as gin. As soon as it gets to June, July you need 'floppy' weather, the wind out and a flop on the sea, little blows, movement, waves four or five foot high coming on the beach to keep the fish in the bay. You prayed for 'July Regatta' weather. If it stayed fine too long the mackerel would clear the whitebait and they'd be gone. They come back but it takes a long time. That's the saying: 'fine weather no fish'.

The only way you can say it's a good year is if you have the end of April and all of May and June in, that's your good season. Two reasons, one the fish keep better in May; it's cooler so they keep better. The fish are all usually good fish, larger, and the demand is there as it's a new season fish (not anymore), but everyone used to look forward to mackerel in May, so you could catch as much as you liked and get a good price. June, July they don't keep as well as they're building their fats for winter and full of whitebait. If you had a good May you had a good season.

It's hard work, fishing. You'd get to Thursday and you'd have a job to drag your legs upstairs at night, barely put one foot in front of the other. It was the best years of me life though, without doubt, earning a good living on the beach. You loved all that, wouldn't want to be anywhere else. It's in your nature; when you see fish you go and catch fish. When I grew up we didn't have much money. Cecil Lexster asked me to go fishing with him and we had a shot of mullet and we took them to Samways at West Bay and he came back a week later and gave me eleven quid. I said to Dick, 'Father, we got to go to Bridport net factory and get some gear and then we can catch some fish.' I did it for the family. I could see that you have to spend some money to get proper gear and make some money. The rope and corks were expensive. I insisted. We went on and earned some money then for the family. It wasn't easy in those days. Fishing's in your blood, you can't change it, it's in your blood.

Abbotsbury crew pulling up the hose full of mackerel.

There was a lot more competition on the beach back then, more crews and boats. Everyone has a different lifestyle now. If you have a crew down that beach and they know what to do it's a well-oiled machine, second nature. The other side of the fishing is that on that beach when it's fine weather it's alright but when it's rough, that's when the lerrets come in. If you had enough hands you could fish the rougher weather but as the crews got smaller years ago, you had square-sterns and you couldn't fish the weather as well as a lerret. You need a big enough crew to use that lerret and know what they're doing. When you're putting a boat afloat and it's rough, it was Ash Huddy who was the man in charge. Split-second decision when you push that boat in, and the most experienced man with the bottle does that job. Ash, he'd give you a warning and then 'go' and no one hesitates or deviates from his decision right or wrong. The shore crew might have to wade right in to make sure that the boat gets in and out through the breakers. Slightly easier to get ashore than afloat as you haven't got the weight of the seine in the boat. Coming shore if it's nasty you have to throw a heaving line, and then on the heaving line you'd have five people to pull that boat ashore, pick your smooth and pull the boat in the smooth. When you hit the beach everyone's out. If the boat turns over it doesn't matter so much about the boat, but you hit the beach and you get everyone out. One man makes the decisions. Sometimes another wave looms up and they have to let the rope back out, pull off two or three times up against a big wave and pick out another smooth and then everyone has to let it out, not hang on or there's hell to pay. That is a skill to learn over time. When I left school it was my job. You have to get your eye back in on it if you're not doing it everyday, start working the weather to get it back into your head. It's a real dangerous job.

You're always aware anything can happen, like when they turned the boat over and Ashley was underneath. They'd wait twenty minutes sometimes to pick a smooth to get the boat afloat, twenty minutes silent waiting around the boat. It was like that when it was rough.

... *Queen Mary* [lerret], he was on top the beach derelict when I was a boy. One last time I remember there was a nasty swell so we used the lerret to get afloat there, and we shot this big deep seine, might've been fifty foot, and we shot it and I was on the ship end ashore, and as we were bringing the net in there was a nasty big swell and we'd filled the damn thing up all small fish, known as 'joey mackerel', so no good to us anyway. Must have been over a thousand stone full up and there was a pleasure boat along the beach, and Ash went over and told them to stay out of it and that evening they drowned themselves. We saw this boat wrecked in the guts of the sea, and there was nothing we could do as we were up to our necks in it ourselves, such a big bundle of fish, and we couldn't get the fish under control, couldn't get them under control at all, we busted the net and the fish swam. Quite a spring tide. Their boat floated past us, smashed up like matchsticks, big sea flattened the whole thing.

Fishing on the Chesil Beach was so important when you go back. Years back, a wooden boat and seine was an awful lot of money to get together, all made by hand, copper rivets, cotton hand-braided nets. The boat and gear a small fortune. So much so, one of the Ropers says two members of their family went over to Australia in the gold rush in the nineteenth century to get some gold and come back and buy a seine and boat, can you imagine, but if you got a boat you'd easily get a crew together. You could earn a living once you got one, a small fortune perhaps – it was important.

thole-pins and copsea oars,
chances lost and won,
hard rows, seines cut and holed,
drive on sweet mackerel shoal

10

Bexington, Swyre and Pucknowle (The Smugglers!)

> … smuggling, and roguing … is the reigning commerce of all this part of the English coast from the Thames to Land's end.
>
> Daniel Defoe (1726)

Winter. Standing in the West Bexington car park and watching the anglers, I try to imagine this coastline in the late afternoons before electricity, cars and maintained public roadways. Everyone wants to be here today to enjoy a sunny brisk walk and the lure of the dancing horizon. It was not always such an inviting prospect. Life by or near the sea was once perilous, and fear of invasion was a real possibility. Bexington discovered this in the fifteenth century when it was invaded by French pirates, burnt down, and its villagers kidnapped and taken away, never to be seen again. In fact, for a long time, the villages of Swyre and Pucknowle preferred inland safety. This tells us something about the character and attitude of local fishermen and smugglers of the time – hundreds of years of swagger, interdependent community, physical strength, courage and seamanship rope-laddered through the generations alongside a legacy of adventure, misery, desperation and resourcefulness. The ability to manage a large operation, lead large groups of men, and act impulsively and fairly when the need arose runs from the smuggler gangs straight through to modern seiners. 'Every village had the [fishing] crews, it was a big wage subsidy,' Rod tells me, and this might also apply to former fisher-smuggling gangs.

Opposite: On a bench outside the hut, left to right: Wally Randall, Chummy Northover, Charl Randall.

Puncknowle and Swyre, half a mile apart and a mile inland, due north of the Chesil Beach at Bexington, are ancient smuggler villages. I scuttle across the cemetery behind the original crossroads at Puncknowle Bottom, where a stone cross once stood and where now a telephone-kiosk book-swap stands opposite the church. The church itself is on Church Street beside the Manor and has only a small immediate churchyard. In the new graveyard I tightrope sturdy yew roots between which the older gravestones lodge. Lichen obscures the details, leaving only grand head-height ship-at-sea tilted slabs of blotched earthy inks and indistinct carvings, for most slabs are smoothed with weather, no words legible. In this cemetery of St Mary's Church, I find Cheneys, Stevens, Coxes and Lavers… but not who I came for, the Northovers. At home, in the Online Parish Clerk's transcripts of gravestones in the churchyard, I find I have in fact missed five Northover graves.

Uncle Chum told Rod he'd often walked down the green lane from Swyre to Bexington beach early mornings as a boy to take his father and uncles a cold breakfast if they'd been on the beach with herring nets all night. The herring swim at night. Chum's great-uncle was Charles Northover, an infamous local smuggling captain, as were *his* father James and his grandfather James before him. Rod tells me he is proud of his smuggling heritage. Smugglers like Charles Northover (1817–1882) cut a large and romantic figure in hindsight. It is written in the Dorchester prison records on the three occasions that he was charged at the Assizes, that Charles was six feet four inches tall, weathered, with dark hazel eyes and a deep scar on his left forehead. His gang of thirty men were seine fishermen in summer, and in winter dug ditches and drains for local farms.

By the time Charles was smuggling, things were getting desperate out on the cliffs. Smuggling 'free-trade' or the coasting trade had been going on since the early Middle Ages, and actively flourished in Dorset, as along all the coast, in the eighteenth and nineteenth centuries. Taxes on imported goods to fund wars placed a heavy burden on the population rich enough to afford luxury items, and were seen as an opportunity by the most desperate and poorest labourers to use their skills to supplement a meagre living.

A government-commissioned report of 1784 estimated that between two-thirds and four-fifths of tea, spirits, wine, sugar and tobacco sold in the preceding years were contraband, reflecting the heavy tax of up to forty percent on fine goods. Puncknowle and Swyre fishermen would have been at the centre of local action, having expert knowledge of the physical coastline for dangerous landings at night. Dorset historian, Roger Gutteridge, mentions fifteen hundred pounds of contraband goods found stashed in the hedges between Swyre and Bexington in 1737, no doubt along the same green lane that Chummy passed through as he carried breakfast to the herring fishermen in the 1920s.

The year 1822 was a turning point. Customs and Excise services were created to prevent smuggling and cut off the flow of contraband. Preventative or 'preventy' men – mostly out-of-work ex-navy men – were hired to patrol the cliffs. Heavy penalties were introduced to induce turning gang members, including the old threat of pressing men into navy service. This was later abandoned, however, as Dorset fishermen were often rewarded with ratings as excellent seamen rather than punished, though the pressing was a five-year sentence. Transportation and, later, hanging were also a punishment for smuggling offences. There were often violent tussles on the beaches, as mounted riding officers and dragoon guards, preventative cutters, watch-houses and guard boats all hovered.

It was due to such vigilance that the smugglers started sinking their barrels, a practice known as 'sewing the crops', coming back for them later rather than risking a direct landing. Fishermen could legitimately row out and spend time on the water at any time of day and night. The labourers working for the Berwick Manor and others in service in Puncknowle and Swyre lived in poverty. But we do not find evidence of community philanthropy from the Northover gang, as we recorded with Isaac Gulliver of Wimborne (*see* page 156). Many lower orders in the gang did not escape the law easily, and would have been whipped and imprisoned in Dorchester, whereas Charles was only fined. He died a wealthy man in 1882, leaving a large Devon farmhouse and estate.

As the fishermen, coastguards and preventative Excise officers were induced by threats and cash-bribes, more smugglers were indicted at the Dorchester Assizes after 1824, and more smuggler goods captured and recovered, for which preventy men were generously rewarded with cash.

Levi Henry John Northover ('Uncle Chum or Chummy') was born in Puncknowle on July 18, 1907. At the harvest festival in 1907 and each year in Puncknowle, a long string of 'fine mackerel' was suspended across the chancel to celebrate the harvest of the sea. After serving in the Navy during the Second World War, Chummy went on to work in the docks at Weymouth and became a successful seine fisherman every other hour of his waking days, bringing wealth and community to himself and his crews until he retired in 1980.

Born just out of the Victorian era, Chum, Ash, Louis, Fred, Ted Hardman, are all men we catch a glimpse of at a distance, from another era, another mould, value system and context.

Chummy and his eight brothers and sisters were a tight-knit band. From Puncknowle he moved to Portland then Chickerell, and once there, he was near the roar and call of beach. I hear from Rex that, 'well yes, fishing was a massive part of his life, but very much a business to him. He was good at it, very good, had a lot of knowledge.' Chum always knew when to launch... 'Something told him this was the time' (Barbara Condliffe, 2011). We can't know the effect that war had on him. He had been on the minesweepers, lost his brother, Mckenna, in a torpedoed submarine. He was sober and disciplined. 'He never smoked, he never drank, he never swore and one of his favourite things to say was that he'd never been into a pub in his life. Ironic, as he ended up in lots of fishing photos all over the walls of The Lugger at Chickerell,' says Rex Ireland.

'At the time he seemed stern, authoritarian. Looking back now, he was amazing. He had a huge garden he looked after, chickens and

June 14

134 ftw Mack
12 ft Mullet
8 ft Salmon

Chummy
J Randall
W Randall
T Beale
B D alley
J Stevens
S Payne
M Pugh
P Pugh mate
D Marshallsay
Toby " " "

Steve Randall
a Aaron
M Baker
E Marshallsay } Boys

From Chummy's account books, a list of Park Wall and catch one June 14th.

lawns, he ran the fishing, made and repaired the nets, looked after the boats and had a job at Weymouth Docks. He was a complete bachelor,' Rex tells me about Uncle Chum, remembered as a young boy, over several summer holidays. Most of what I learn of Chum and other seining captains like him along Chesil are from account books recording the catches, and memories of endless summers of fish by crew and young relatives, all of whom looked up to him. Such competitive and serious characters as these captains are celebrated in faded Kodak trophy photos, men shaped by and utterly connected to the context of their time with attitudes and values formed by wartime and post-war hardship, material and social ambitions.

One rare glimpse of Chum is in the fragment of memory handed down by his sisters Marjorie and Barbara, who recounted how Chum, on leave in New York during the war, had came home with suitcases of dresses and stockings for them.

Uncle George Randall (1888–1970) and many other fishermen did like a drink. 'George would light a fire then go and have a few pints in The Lugger and come home to his thatched cottage behind the pub, only to find the fire was now halfway across the main and only downstairs room. He'd collect driftwood logs from beach and light the whole trunk and just push the trunk into the fire as it burned down.' Rex also tells me, 'Old George used to tell stories about ghosts and fishing capers and smugglers and would always stay in the kitchen, never joined everyone in the front room at lavish family Christmas parties,' at the house Chum had built, *Ja'stan*, and where he lived with his spinster sister, Aunt Gwen, who kept the books.

The nave of Puncknowle's St Mary's church, now the vestry, was once known as the Bexington aisle, a small space, with a small framed notice telling the story of how a French raid in the 1440s destroyed the Church of St Giles, which stood near the sea, and the entire Saxon village of Bexington, with the French taking many of the villagers away. The decision not to restore St Giles or the village was made by the Earl of Wiltshire and the Abbot of Abbotsbury. The Rector of Puncknoll was required to 'celebrate in the chancel of Bexington once a week and on St Giles' day.' This may account for one 'Robert Northover of Bexington' who died in 1698 in Swyre, and many migrations up the road. Bexington families were accommodated into Puncknowle and carried their knowledge, seine and smuggling secrets with them. Many Puncknowle villagers by the mid-eighteenth century were seining fishermen in summer and would have taken that old green lane down from Swyre to the beach to launch their lerrets.

In the *Dundee Courier* on Monday, July 30, 1923, there is an article about a smuggler ghost haunting the village of Swyre, a tall 'seafaring man in uniform with luminous buttons'. The report details the local belief that a skeleton found on the foreshore by a labourer and left to lie in a dry ditch 'hidden by weeds and long grass', a hundred years before, was the body of a local smuggler involved in a fight with Excise men. The villagers were busy looking for the remains to offer a proper burial and quiet the ghost – 'he has been so busy lately and rattled his scabbard so fiercely at belated villagers that they have decided to quiet him.'

Nothing like fear to keep people away, but there is more to this report than a warning. A bell trembles in the collective memory of wrongs unforgotten. This skeleton remains unlucky and unnamed in history, stepped over in haste.

Cargoes were passed up-country to smuggler handlers like Rob Channing of West Hatch in Somerset, an infamous innkeeper and coal haulier with a wharf, whose empty return waggons carried contraband to Wales and Bristol, 'whilst the Excise men were still combing the coastal shores'. In 1940, it was said that 'farmers and all men alike were in league with Rob, 'twouldn't 'av' paid to be otherwise both from fear of un and favour of un. 'Twere no sense in opposing un. Them as did – they 'ad darkly – disappeared!' (*Western Gazette*, December 27, 1940).

There are other mentions of smugglers in violent scuffles. James Hatton of Loders who was shot at Burton Freshwater by a preventative officer, died in 1839, which was judged by an inquest to be 'justifyable homicide'. James was discovered in the small hours by five or more Puncknowle labourers and fishermen who just happened to be passing Kettle Bridge in Burton Bradstock at that hour, and who sent to Bridport for a doctor. Patrick Farrell, the boatman, also making money as a preventy officer said, 'What I did was in the execution of my duty. The men had sticks.' The general instruction was for officers to use their arms in 'self-defence to prevent a landing', but in the dark, with the gangs loose and hardy, the mood was tense and twitchy.

Entrepreneur smuggler-fishermen such as Charles Northover were good with figures, a leader commanding many men, and ambitious to make a better life whatever the means. He may have been inspired by Isaac Gulliver, who in the mid to late eighteenth century ran a mob of legitimate businesses as a cover for a successful smuggling organisation, including owning a haulier firm with a full-time retinue of men to serve buyers in London. He invested in land and property, and even purchased land at Eggardon Heath in order to plant trees on the summit as a mark for sailors. He was a good man from the records, giving to the poor and sharing his wealth. When Gulliver died in 1822 (a churchwarden of Wimborne Minster) he was very wealthy, had risen in stature from humble beginnings, and known across Dorset as a people's hero, though some believe his smuggling operations were a government-sponsored spying operation, to keep an eye on the French.

Smuggling, fishing and poaching were all a means of livelihood and advancement in small coastal communities, when other avenues were closed. No doubt the severity of laws passed in 1816 emboldened local coasting trade; it was proclaimed that 'any person loitering within five miles of the sea coast ... suspected to assist in the running of goods, is to be brought before a justice ... to be whipped and kept to hard labour for one month.'

Among the documents I read at the Dorset History Centre Archive, one day when the car park was flooded and my boots also, was a rare and wonderful snapshot, *A Description of the Inhabitants of the Cottages of the Parish of Swyre and Berwick* 1869, written by the local teacher. The names of some of the parishioners are their given names, plus as in the case of Henry Northover, 'commonly called 'Philly', the names assumed for smuggling to avoid detection.

Also mentioned were smugglers Junker, Arnold, Dick Lawyer, Wild Boy, Jack Caddy, Cribber and our friend Charles Northover, their Captain, at this time aged fifty-two. And a damning report it is of him: 'a selfish and covetous man and does not care by what means he can enrich himself.' In addition to smuggling activity, barely disguised by his swagger and pride, the report goes on to relate the story that, 'when his mother died, she had some money which he secured for himself, and deprived the rest of the family of their proper shares. He had a sister, who had a little money, and he persuaded her to make it over to his son Charles, and after that she was kept by the parish.' I'm shocked by this last. Humiliation and destitution probably awaited this sister once she'd lost her independence. Exhausted by child-bearing and labour and living in poverty-induced hopelessness, women in the report are chastised for lack of cleanliness and good order. More than one small cottage had upwards of nine people living in it. As I drive past the cottages, such basic and awful conditions are, thankfully, hard to imagine.

A side-step inland and back along the secretive and hidden green lane down into dark nights, ghosted by desire and hopes of a better life, and we emerge back again on the beach.

Shire Hall by *Anne Brown*

Shire Hall in Dorchester was the Crown Court of Dorset from 1797 to 1955 and opened as an historic courthouse museum in 2018. It held the Quarter sessions four times a year, trying non-capital crimes, and unlike the Assizes, these were overseen by untrained Magistrates with local connections. The comprehensive and intact court and prison records held at the Dorset History Centre give voice to many stories of ordinary working people who stood in the docks. Witchcraft was still being heard in court in 1824, though it was the witch accuser who was on trial and found guilty. An outbreak of duck theft in Wimborne, highway robbery in Blandford, poaching just about everywhere, and, of course, smuggling all feature prominently in the records.

Looking at lists of smugglers in the prison and court records, we see patterns emerge. Certain place names, scenes of crime, surnames and occupations recur frequently. Ages are more varied. Swyre and Puncknowle are particularly interesting; the same families and the same first names are used and re-used, but identifying who is who and how they are connected is like untangling fishing nets. What we can see are patterns of juries hesitating to convict, with surprisingly lenient, as well as surprisingly severe, fines and punishments, and the same individuals from the same places come up the stairs from the holding cells to the courtroom time after time after time.

The Charles Northover mentioned earlier in this chapter was baptised in Swyre on January 19, 1817, into a family of smugglers: father, grandfathers, uncles, brothers and cousins. He first appeared in the prison register on December 20, 1828, at the age of twelve, along with the thirteen-year-old Henry Northover (likely his cousin), for stealing turnips. Both were sentenced to one month's hard labour in Dorchester Gaol. There were no children's units at that time. The age of criminal responsibility was seven years old, so they were effectively adults.

In 1847, we see Charles in court again. At the age of thirty years old, a single man and a fisherman, he was arrested in Corscombe and charged with smuggling, presumably en route inland with smuggled goods. He was fined £25 and sent to prison for three calendar months, again with hard labour.

After a remarkably long interlude where it would be incautious to assume he had learnt his lesson and was no longer smuggling, Charles was once again arrested far inland:

'[He] was charged with having in his possession nearly two gallons of brandy on which duty had not been paid. A policeman met the defendant on the night of the 23rd December (1870) on the highway at Frome Vauchurch, near Maiden Newton, observed that he carried a large basket, made an inspection of its contents, thinking to find game (pheasants, rabbits or ducks), and discovered brandy. As Mr Grieve, collector of customs at Weymouth, did not press the case (make a proper case in court), defendant [Charles Northover] was fined in the mitigated penalty of £1 18s. and costs, the brandy forfeited [taken from Charles Northover].'

Twenty-three years between crimes – had Charles Northover really not been smuggling during this time or had he just not been caught? Had he been caught but not pursued? Why did Mr Grieve, collector of customs at Weymouth, not pursue the case? All interesting questions, but not ones whose answers lie in the prison or court records, or the archives. The good smugglers leave very little trace of their work.

11

Burton Beach and West Bay

Sarah Acton with Nancy (b. 1930), Ricky (b. 1963) and Tracey Gape (b. 1972)

Sarah: *I have read about a couple of drownings of seine fishermen back in the day.* The Bridport News *reports two incidents at Burton. One in 1880 was a drinking trip to West Bay and the boat capsized, three drowned. John Camel survived because he could swim but most crews couldn't swim, though interestingly these were the first drownings of seine fishermen I'd read about. Then in 1899, thirty-three-year-old Charles Gape, who, it says, was captain of a Puncknowle boat, after shooting the net, dropped off four crewmen, went back to keep the boat, and lost his balance. 'The boat was between 20 and 30 yards from the shore.' The coroner's inquest told off the crew, 'running such risks as fishermen and not the common sense to learn this simple and ordinary precaution... to be able to swim was the first and necessary knowledge.' The inquest also sadly said that 'life was not gone when he was brought ashore,' but no one knew how to resuscitate.*

Ricky: Yeh, Charles Gape was our great-grandfather, my grandfather Bertie's father. Bertie must've been very young when that [drowning] happened. Now I was always led to believe that the net caught on the buttons of Charles's tweed coat as he was throwing the seine over and pulled him; that's what we heard all these years. That he got caught up in the net and then they had to drag the net in to bring him in. He drowned before they could get him up, see. I've heard

Opposite: Phil Hutchings with horn carved by Thomas Hutchings, fisherman of Burton Bradstock – the horn was used to tell villagers that the catch was being landed (courtesy of Pat Hutchings).

all these years and thought no different. Des's [Desi Gape, Ricky's father] brother was called Charles, may have been a connection.

Nancy: He couldn't swim, that was the problem. They lived at Puncknowle. We're all related with the Lavers, Millers and all the old fishing families. Not a close relationship.

So your ancestors all fished?

Ricky: You couldn't say it didn't go back to seventeen or sixteen hundreds, or even fourteen hundreds? We won't ever really know.

Nancy: It wasn't written down much, you wouldn't pass on or record information further down than two generations, they would never have thought of writing it down like that.

Were you from Burton, Nancy?

Nancy: No, I'm from Bradninch in Devon and my dad used to own a farm with his brother and they sold the business and my dad worked for other farmers, Mr Chick at Compton Valance approached my dad to get the rabbit population under control. He come up to Dorset to farm at Chick's farm. Des came out of the army and went to work for my father.

And your husband, Des, was fishing all this time?

Nancy: Yes, he was always fishing. Then he went to work at Samways driving the long distances to Billingsgate and Lowestoft up with fish and back with crab, quite long distances. They used to sell fish off the beach. He was very popular. He always put in a little bit more, you see.

Ricky: Sprat to catch the mackerel... so Dad's crew was Tommy Parr, Chuckle Parr, Barry Holmwood, Stuart Tattershall, Little Man, someone House from Winterbourne Steepleton, that's just who I can remember straight off.

Seine boats at Burton Hive (courtesy of Humphrey Bickford).

Nancy: He was brought up fishing and was always there on the beach, mainly the seine, then later feathers. We had the seine at our house for a long time.

Ricky: We even had another seine made in the '80s, me brother and my dad, Maurice Youngs and others. The seining had dropped off when we moved back to Burton. We'd just go out and hook them with feathers. Then we had two boats made for the beach. One was the *Why-Not* and there was *Nancy-Clarice* for lobster pots under the cliffs. The guy at West Bay made us the seine, Rex Walmington… not sure, did he make nets? Anyway, we had another go at it. Burton was getting a bit rocky then, so we went down Cogden. We never had much success with that net, but we were doing it again in the late '80s, a smaller crew, more family. When they did the seine down before I can't really remember too much, except I remember you used to get soaked, and I used to chuck the pebbles alongside the arms to keep the fish back in. Important job, you had to watch the waves.

Nancy: It all used to smell so much.

Ricky: When you pull the arms in on the seine, just before the last arm reaches the net that comes into the beach, the fish have a chance to escape, especially if you're walking down with the tide. If you've got big tides that net would flow on down, and we used to chuck pebbles to scare 'em back 'cos the arm had not quite come ashore, you see, and they weren't caught in the arms back into the purse so they could get out in big droves, so my dad used to say to me, 'Scoot 'em in, so they go thhhrrrr', and all of a sudden they'd fly backwards. That was my job. I expect you've heard that before?

Tracey: They were doing the seine last summer inside the harbour at West Bay… Gary Copp. We could see it all looking down, first-hand and right on top of it.

I know that your husband was a keen fisherman, Nancy. I heard he was out fishing when you were pregnant?

Nancy: That's a story that is. This was early morning and he'd had a call to get down to the beach as the mackerel were straying. We were living at Kingston Russell. I knew something was happening with the baby, it was number six, and he said ring this number when you're ready, and he went fishing. I called this man and he had to go up on the cliff and wave for him to come in. He went up and waved to Des and he had to come in off the water and come up to Kingston to take me to Dorchester. It might've been Cut Thorner. There was no panic really, he (points to Ricky) didn't arrive until teatime. I imagine he went straight back out to fishing after that. I didn't mind him doing the fishing at all. It was in their blood, wasn't it, and with all of his friends.

Ricky: Wasn't there always something to eat and some extra coins… what you could earn was what you could get, no welfare.

Nancy: They were all good friends, different sort of men. Generations change don't they…

Ricky: They were very together and they all liked each other. If there was anything going on, well, men used to sort things out quick, never any tension or anything like that.

Ricky: It was in 1963, Dad always told me it was the best year for mackerel. Obviously, there was the cold winter of 62–63, then July '63, he used to say, what a great year it was for mackerel, always used to tell me that all the time.

Nancy: They used to catch so many they didn't know what to do with them. He knew all about fishing, didn't he, his father used to do it.

Ricky: Did it right up until he couldn't go out no more.

Tracey: You're the last one now, fishing off Burton beach.

Pete (b. 1946) and Pearl Parsons (b. 1947), Pat (b. 1950) and Phil Hutchings (b. 1948)

Sarah: *So we're looking at photos of these seine boats on Burton Hive.*

Pat: Yes, that's my father's boat, the *Why-Not*, a seine boat. There was a sailing brig called the *Why-Not*, built in 1849, owned by Bridport ship-owners. Most of Phil's ancestors were mariners. Nearly all of the men going back up the line were mariners at sea. In 1881, well the *Why-Not* was wrecked at Peterhead off Scotland. It had half the family and male relations on board of that generation. All perished, and some of the widows and children moved in together into one cottage in Donkey Lane and had to live off the parish after that. And there were no benefits in those days. They used to make nets and help with the fish on the beach. All Phillip's family have lived in the village forever. This timeline for the Hutchings family goes back to the seventeenth century but I couldn't go back further as the mice ate the parish records. The mariner Thomas Hutchings made the horn you can see there, with a scrimshaw image of the brig *Why-Not* on it and a mackerel there... So they would blow the horn to signal mackerel.

Pat: They'd stand on the cliff and blow it. There's a knack to blowing it. And that was to tell the villagers the fish was in to help process it all along the beach. It was used in the 1800s and early 1900s. They used to bring in so much fish. Our fishermen were part-timers, not professionals like up at Abbotsbury at this time.

Pat: This is Alfie Hutchings [points to a photograph], one of his boats was called the *Why-Not*. He also owned another boat, the *Shirley*, named after Phillip's sister. There were lots of boats operating down there at the time.

Pat: And Desi, my father, also had a boat called the *Why-Not*. There's always been a *Why-Not* boat down on the beach of some description.

So, Pete and Phil, were both of your families fishermen?

Pete: No, not mine. I was farming up at Northfield Farm, dairy farmer, moved up to the farm across the road, moved about, the'm all gone now. Used to mow the grass in the evenings after tea. Then used to go fishing with Phil's father. Phil's family always fished. When we were young we used to stand behind the net to stop the big catch from getting out, just holding on the bow. Sprats and mackerel – we'd sled them up the beach on galvanised to the lorry. The catches were so big. We used to sit for hours boxing them up. If we didn't tell stories about what'd been buried we got an extra bob or two. Phil was a builder and went haymaking.

Phil: You did anything to earn money. You just had to go and work. Work day jobs, work before and after, just to live. You learnt on the job. If you didn't pay attention you got a smack around the ear.

Did you go out on the boat?

The Shirley seine boat off Burton Bradstock, with left to right: Dennis Bullock, Alfie Hutchings, Chris Hutchings, Phil Hutchings (courtesy of Pat Hutchings).

Pete: Yeh, always the seining. We didn't have feathers – until an old man from the village, Dicker, went down to Cornwall and came back and told everyone about them. They didn't believe him to start. We'd go down five in the morning for seining and Pearl and Dawn would pack and sell the fish off the beach and we'd go out again. Ours was hobby fishing.

Phil: Where we lived down in the village, the bloke next door had a lorry 'specially for fish. Cut Thorner. They called him Cutty as he was always cutting the price. The only person in the village with a telephone. Before the telephone they used this horn up on the cliff. Before our time though.

Pete: There was Dicker Thorner and Bert Thorner his brother; they shared a boat. He made a boat in his garden.

Pat: Then there was Alfie, who came from a long line of fishermen. They would've had several boats over time. There was lerret on the

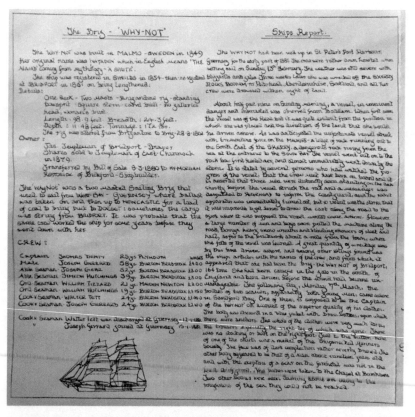

Extract of Phil Hutchings' family tree regarding the sinking of the brig, the *Why-Not*, 1881 (courtesy of Pat Hutchings).

beach; they used those for seining more than the square-end boats. He might've inherited a boat and he bought one out the back of the war. Simeon, Phil's grandfather, was a full-time fisherman and he also had a guest house in the village during the war, Vine House, opposite the Anchor. Phil is the last of the Hutchings fishermen, and my two brothers, Chris and Ricky, are the last of the Gape fishermen. They've had a winch down there on Burton beach for a long time, now replaced; they have to have this, and rollers and planks across the beach or nothing moves. You have to help it along, they're heavy boats. The beach was full of boats at the turn of the last century but there are half-a-dozen working boats we remember. Bertie Williams and Stanley bought the fish. Phillip's father was one of the main fishermen. He was a painter an' he had to have a second job. The big crew at Abbotsbury could do it for a living. They were all rivals, of course. About five seines on that beach, five crews. Alfie fished with Dennis Bullock. This was to supplement wages. They were all brought up fishing. All of these people on the family tree lived and died in the village.

Did you have a hut?

Phil: Not like the one at Abbotsbury; they used to live in their hut. We had a small hut for the nets.

Did you move to Burton, Pat?

Pat: Yes, in 1963, we had to move to Burton as my father was on the beach fishing all of the time, so we just had to move here.

So there were a lot of fish?

Pearl: Often too many to handle.

Did you get many other boats coming in?

Pat: More at West Bay; that's a tidal harbour. They'd have a job to come on Burton beach, you had to know the Chesil well and the shelves of the beach. When to go out, when to come in. It's easier to come in and out at West Bay. It was mainly the villagers fishing off of Burton beach, a village of fishermen. This is why the fish were so important, to eat, to preserve in salt and eat in winter and they sold it. They lived off it. It was all free except they had to work for it. It fed the family and you could sell to holidaymakers – that was lucrative even from the 1930s or 40s. In our time, Saturdays and Sundays the men went fishing and we sold the fish on the beach.

Pearl: People started to ask and we said, 'Yeh we'll sell 'em.' Was money to go out in the evening.

Was there much competition?

Phil: Yeh, they used to squabble, yes. Occasionally Aish would come from Abbotsbury and have damn great nets and he'd go around our seines with his nets; a lot of that went on. There's a lot of rocks about an' if you got stuck on 'em you had to lift your nets. They had the fish you would've got. There was some language and few fisty-cuffs, perhaps, but it was all done by then, the shot was ruined. But generally there wasn't many others on the beach, only us locals there a lot of the time.

You'd drive down...

Pete: Just a road down to the beach. Horse and cart used to go right down for gravel and you'd see the marks on the road.

So what was particular about Burton fishing?

Phil: It was all family boats and the fishing was a necessity. They lived off it. It was all run proper with a book.

Pat: The seine nets were smaller and small boats. Our Dad had a crew of up to eight to launch and pull it in because of the Chesil pebbles.

Pete: Greased the bottom of the boat and planks to roll the boat up the beach. People in the village came down to help pull the boats up.

Pat: We had to wait to get the boat out in the waves. There's been wrecks off Burton beach, treacherous it can be. Wouldn't like to tell you how many holidaymakers have lost their lives swimming.

Pete: We was down on the beach years back and 'owd Bertie Williams said, 'Tell those boys there don't go out in that sea today and not you go out in there either today.' Those boys dived in under the water, swimming, and washed up down near Lyme Regis nearly a week later.

Pat: It's down to the tides, the storms, the pull from underneath when there's a storm; you don't go anywhere near the water.

Pearl: The cliff has altered so much in the last fifty years. Where we used to picnic is not there anymore, it was miles from the edge. Almost halved.

Phil: Certain areas where there are rocks and you can't shoot your seine where the rocks are. If the nets are fouled you have to lift your nets off it and you'll lose your catch. Whitebait would bring the mackerel in so they didn't have to go far. You'd walk with the net. When the tides was running strong you'd have to move the arm, and walk with the tide along the beach together and gradually get down the beach until the net is practically in, there's an art to it.

Phil: There was nothing else. Holidays straight down the beach and every day in season after work. We've known each other since school. Don't know how many of us who's left now, not many of us.

Pete: My sisters were mending the nets, everyone involved. The fish started disappearing. Everyone started doing it and when the sprats came in, the sprats came in like flies. West Bay, you couldn't even see it for the red haze. They look red with the sun on, noses are red. They call them 'reds', the sprats, thousands down there. The crews would come from miles away to catch them. Sent them up Netherbury as fish manure or mixed up as cow food when there was such a glut. Still there but not in the amount. Then the factory ships started out to sea in the '70s.

Phil: They could come back now but not in the same quantities as they were then. You used to see mackerel driving the whitebait and they'd wash up all along the beach, swam straight up the beach; well, you don't see that anymore.

Richard Larcombe (b. 1948)

We lived in West Bay right near the beach. As there was no housing after the war, we lived there in what was a holiday chalet. Several families lived in these chalets on stilts so the sea would wash underneath. Then we moved back to Bradpole when I was five and Dave was three. Our family came from Mapperton – farmers on my father's side and my mother's side from Bradpole. My father was the only one went into fishing. Fish and rabbits, what he caught, were our mainstay diet. My father used to fire the rocket for the ship rescues with the breaches buoy; they used to practise off the cliff.

Most of the boats stayed on the beach then, above the high-tide line. You always needed half-a-dozen crew just to get the boat out on the greased planks. I went out later with my father, Archie, Bert Miller, Bert Neale, Pat Day. All part-timers. We went out on Clifford Samway's boat, *Yogi Bear*.

If we were under the East Cliff it was quite a long way to haul the fish to the lorry, but on the West side of the beach you could park on the front, so less far to carry. We seined from both sides. There was always rocks all the way along. The West side is better from the end of the prom to the pier but there's more rocks from there to Eype side, an outcrop there from which the table rock sticks out. From the pier to the cliff on the east side was the clearest bit, then from the cliff towards Freshwater was probably more rocky. You can get a terrible drop out there. The shingle only starts on our East side, the West side we're more pebbles.

It was hard hauling the fish up the beach. There were several crews fishing. We were young enough then that muscles didn't seem to ache so much. We didn't go further than a third of the way along to Freshwater as we would've had to haul the fish back.

Samways supplied the seine nets and the boat and organised the buyer before he started his business an' sold his own fish. If it was, say, ten stone, not a vast amount, we could sell those off the fish box on the beach. You could make good money at the weekends with holidaymakers.

We could catch a seine net full of mackerel and sprats. The nets got bigger and bigger as the years went by. The last net Clifford had made could hold ten tonne of fish. If you caught that lot you'd be all day to get it up the beach. Sometimes such a glut of sprats. They are good to eat but in those numbers they weren't for human consumption; they went to fish manure or something. It was quite a spectacle really with a big catch.

Once we had such a catch that we towed it from East beach into the harbour and unloaded it onto the small harbour. When the shipyard was there it was where they launched the ships. We've tipped the boat over several times.

The price for feathered mackerel, well, we used to get eight shillings a stone then two shillings grant from the government, but if you did that you'd declare your earnings and pay tax at the time. I was too young to pay tax but I fished with a full-time fisherman and he used to claim it back, but the boat had to be registered. Somewhere further up Chesil Beach on the other side of the beach. Well, how were they ever going to check?

The older fishermen all liked the pub. It was social for them as well as money, a real community. My father and the rest of the crew enjoyed it and it was extra cash, money to spend in the pub. They really enjoyed it though, I know that.

Dave Larcombe (b. 1951)

I used to disappear for the day fishing soon as I was old enough, with my sandwiches. I was about fifteen, maybe earlier, and I used to creep down the beach, and I'd give a hand and say: 'Can I get in the boat, mister?' West Bay was the place to go, nothing in the town. It's changed completely, now. I loved the beach.

There used to be a beach in the middle of the harbour. We all learnt to swim off there as it was part of the harbour. Later they dredged it out to get more boats in there. It was shallow and sheltered. We'd use the inner tubes from the garage as rings. We used to go swimming in between the old piers, diving off. Lots of smaller boats, two-man boats then. They were all tied up in the harbour around the edge or pulled up out of the water.

I had a rod for angling, and we dug out the bait, the ragworm. We'd use pebbles with a hole or a spark plug for a weight. Catching little pout-whiting, couple home for cat. Father used to go down and I'd go with him if the weather was nice when he finished work.

Later, he used to work for Clifford Samways. He sold the fish, which started on a handcart at West Bay, and then Clifford had a market stall with a wooden-fronted counter and my father used to go and sell at Sturminster Newton, Sherborne, Castle Cary, Dorchester, Yeovil, market days, all the different days of the week. Clifford used to keep live lobsters and crabs in an aerated tank and father would drive them to Billingsgate overnight iced down in boxes. They had to be sold live. Used to take ages to get there. They will live a little while, the iced boxes wetted down with rags and seaweed.

They'd go out feathering in Clifford's boat with Bert Neale and Pat Day. You'd have a hand line with twelve feathers. You had to watch out for the four-pound weight dragging over the side. I've seen times when someone or other got all tangled up with the hooks in their hands. You'd go out further, perhaps two miles with the feathers. They went out to what they'd call the Sewers Buoy, or they'd be just off the end of the pier, not quite near enough for seining.

Ours was a flat-backed boat. We used to have two oars on the boat, not four, and the seine would sit on the back seat with someone to throw and two of us rowing as fast as possible to get the seine round. Clifford or father would sit at the back and throw the seine. There's a certain way of throwing it off the boat and a certain way of packing it back on the boat. Once you went round with the seine there was a rope with a buoy at the back and you'd look at the buoy to see if the fish were going into the net. Clifford'd be peeling the seine out and jump out on the beach first and we'd go back out with the boat until the bunt end came in and they'd pull the boat up and I'd end up jumping in the net to scoop them out, all covered in scales.

I was caught bunking off school only when Mr Board the inspector from the school would come round and mother would get the report then.

Clifford and father used to go across to The George and play darts on a Friday night or cards on a Sunday morning; they played Brag, I think. I'd get here to help and they'd go off. We'd have lunch at two in the afternoon on a Sunday. He'd get up to the markets at half six in the mornings and he'd get the regulars queueing at the stall there by eight in the morning. They used to get rid of a fair bit of fish. At Gore Cross Samways have a factory and the fish shop at West Bay. Sometimes I'd go off with father hawking the fish in the villages out the back of the van, next to nothing then. We'd shout: 'Fresh mackerel, fresh West Bay mackerel.' Anywhere we could think of driving around. We'd have greaseproof to wrap them up in, or some women, it used to be mostly women, might come up with a plate.

There was always a chance of going out. We used to go and seine at Eype and row back from there. If it was a small catch it wasn't worth getting the lorry over there, so you'd load up the boat and row back and hope the waves didn't roll in over the back as you came into the harbour, to get off the front of it.

You used to listen to the forecast or look at the seaweed or pinecones to see what weather was coming. It could change down here, blowing and then an hour later it's blown off. Wind blowing off the land was better. We'd sometimes go out under the cliff line to shield us; out in the open water you were exposed to all sorts.

You'd go out just before the tide goes down and fish over the tide rising and lowering again. We've got a fish finder now but they're all swimming the same way; they must go the other way sometimes.

I remember the boat builders... John Holmes, Cyril Toms, shipwright and carpenter, and boat-builder John Miller at West Bay. There's a slipway in West Bay with a bench and a vice on. That's where they did the woodwork. It's still there. Johnny would whittle bits for the boats in winter on the quayside. When it all went to fibreglass they all became builders.

The beach has changed so much on both sides now. The old groins used to cut the waves up more so the waves in the harbour come in different. Then it used to be a gradual slope on the gravel side on west beach. The other side with the pier and rocks they put in, well, you can't get the nets round the rocks. It just seemed to stop.

I still go down on the pier, or fish off the beach and have shares in a boat. We give them away these days, bit of a pastime. You get to know the people down there and I've been doing it all my life. Used to carry the rod in the van as a carpenter and get out the van at Abbotsbury and catch a few. I didn't need the fish but I couldn't help myself. Some evenings it's peaceful down the harbour, and to see the fish coming in like before... I might sit there in the pouring rain. Anybody else would've gone, but I might catch something.

When men have left their children staid,
And they again have boy and maid,
O, can they know, as years may roll,
Their children's children, soul by soul?
If this with souls in heaven can be,
Do my fore-elders know of me?

from 'My fore-elders' by William Barnes

The Legacy of *Littlesea* and *Vera*
Gail McGarva

When I first met *Vera* the lerret she was quietly wintered up at
Langton Herring on a little patch of green protected from the harsh
weathers. She was some way inland from her old fishing ground of
the Chesil Beach. She was beamy and curvaceous and she sang out
a song of the pebbles, the mackerel and the scree. In their heyday
of the 1800s, it is believed over a hundred lerrets could be seen
perched along the expanse of Chesil Beach. In 2009, by contrast,
only a handful remained. *Vera*, owned by Ian Reeder, was built
in 1923 by Jack Wills at Ferry Bridge for Tom Randall and was
named after Tom's daughter *Vera*, born in the same year.

As a traditional wooden-boat-builder, I am passionate about
the working boats all along our coastline, each with a story to tell
about their communities and their shores. My specialist area is the
building of replicas, or, as I prefer to call them, 'daughterboats',
breathing life into a new generation of traditional boats. They are
not static museum pieces but expressions of living history.

These working boats are strong and robust and yet the lines are
truly elegant, a beautiful interweaving of form and function. No
shape of a boat has come to be by chance but is perfectly evolved
to carry out her task and perform in her waters. The lerret is a rare
example of a traditional working boat whose identifying features
have remained essentially unchanged for generations, crafted
to withstand the challenges of the Chesil Beach. The lerret is a
double-ended, flat-floored, beamy clinker boat, her hull perfectly
shaped to be launched from the top of the scree, fully loaded with
oars, nets and crew, and fly down the pebbles into the sea. She is
meant for these waters.

Opposite: The launch of *Littlesea* (photo by Martin Haswell).

I first heard of the lerrets from Rex Ireland and his mother, Marjorie, whose older brother was Chummy Northover. They shared their memories of Chummy, the Park Wall crew and his fleet of lerrets and it became clear there was a rich and evocative history in the story of the lerret. It was also clear that this vessel type was in danger of extinction. Many of the working boats along the coastline of Britain are under threat and sadly the stories and memories they hold are being lost as the generations pass.

In 2010, I decided to apply to the Queen Elizabeth Scholarship Trust for a scholarship to build a replica of *Vera* in order to preserve the lineage of the lerret. In the building of this daughterboat I also sought to preserve the art of boat-building 'by eye' by taking the lines from the motherboat and building without the use of designer drawings and construction plans. My mentor for the project was retired boat-builder Roy Gollop, who has built boats by eye all his working life. Building the daughterboat enabled these skills to be passed on from one generation of builder to the next.

We took references of *Vera*'s hull shape in order to create three building frames for the construction of the daughterboat. We recorded the shape of the hull at the midships section and at two points in the bow and stern where the hull changed most dramatically in shape. We used a simple and yet effective device, a cross-spall beam with a series of perpendicular 'fingers', spaced at six-inch intervals, to assist in the recording of the hull shape.

The Boat Building Academy in Lyme Regis, where I had originally trained, very kindly offered to house the build of the new boat. Here we plotted the recorded dimensions onto a grid, drawn on a whitewashed sheet of hardboard. The body plan of *Vera* at these three key positions was produced with the use of fairing battens, in readiness for the creation of the three building frames. Similarly recorded measurements taken from *Vera* to capture the rake of the stems were plotted on a whiteboard and again with the use of battens, templates were created. The three key stations along the centre-line structure gave crucial guidance as to the very particular shape of the lerret hull, most specifically with a pronounced fullness in the aft section to give extra buoyancy when launching through the surf of the Chesil Beach.

With the construction of this new-generation lerret, we wished to reflect the essence of the motherboat while acknowledging that the daughterboat has her own unique character. The daughterboat was to be called *Littlesea*, a name inspired by my conversations with Marjorie Ireland, who told me that this was the local name for the Fleet. *Littlesea*'s planking echoes those of *Vera*'s, with twelve planks aside of 3/8" elm. As ever, with any clinker build, the lines of the planking are eyed in, to ensure that the boat is 'sweet on the eye'. The sheerline, the line of the top plank, reflects the characteristic rise in the stern of all lerrets. The backbone is made of oak, with the stems shaped from great crooks of oak with the most beautiful marbled grain. The sternpost projects eight inches above the sheerline, as it is here that the start rope would be coiled, ready for use at sea.

Alongside Roy Gollop as mentor, two other loyal men and true, Dave Govier and Roy Tolley, accompanied me on the journey of building *Littlesea*. I will remain ever appreciative of their time, commitment and skill. It was the most fantastic process, shaping this most curvaceous and beamy clinker boat; a complete contrast to the slim, sleek forms of the Cornish pilot gigs I have built.

A group of young people joined us for steaming and 'timbering out' *Littlesea*'s ribcage. These young people were 'excluded' from mainstream education and attended a unit in Weymouth. The process of timbering out with them was an absolute joy. The results of steaming and bending are so immediate and so visually rewarding. The ribcage grew as we all worked together as a team, bending and persuading the timbers into shape. The young people could not believe how pliable the steaming oak was as I urged them to bend it just a little bit more in order to ease the timber into the belly of the boat. We were all euphoric to see our completed 'whaleboat'.

Later in the build I was able to invite trainee boat-builders and members of the local community to come and shape a knee for the boat. The knees are the oak components that support the seats or 'thwarts' in the boats. All the knees hold the names of their shapers,

Vera at Langton Herring (photo by Keith Pritchard).

stamped onto the inside face of the knee, hidden from the world but strong in the memory of the people who made them.

People from the local community also joined together in the oiling of the boat. Armed with brushes and pots of oil, people joined in the celebration of feeding *Littlesea*'s timber until she was full to the brim, bringing to life the wonderful hues of the elm and oak.

We were also able to invite members of the local community to make the oars for the lerret, with invaluable funding from National Historic Ships. Boat Building Academy lecturer Mike Broome tutored the participants through the whole process, producing a quartet of beautiful oars of Douglas fir with copses of ash.

During the build of *Littlesea*, *Vera*'s owner for over forty years, Ian Reeder, made the hard decision to retire *Vera* from her life at sea and sought somebody to take her on. So in the spring of 2010, I adopted *Vera* – she was given to me as a gift by my dear friend Kerry Maguire. It was wonderful to have the two generations of lerrets coming together when *Vera* joined *Littlesea* in the latter stage of the build.

Littlesea was launched on July 31, 2010, with Marjorie Ireland officially naming the new daughterboat. Marjorie and her sister Barbara Condliffe, along with their sons Rex and Rod, gathered together with many members of the lerret fishing families from all along the Chesil Beach. Many were overwhelmed to see a new lerret being launched, given that the last new one had been built over forty years ago. *Littlesea* was rowed out to sea by the people who had helped shape her. *Vera*, her motherboat, accompanied her, rowed by fishermen who had rowed her in their younger years. This was *Vera's* last day at sea.

During the build of *Littlesea*, many people had come forward with their photographs, articles and stories of the lerrets and it became clear that there was a wonderful story to tell. So I approached the then curator of Lyme Regis Museum, Mary Godwin, with the idea of creating an oral history project to preserve the memories of the lerret fishing communities. With financial support from the Heritage Lottery Fund, we were able to record the voices of people who worked the lerrets and create an oral history archive. Many of these voices speak out in the pages of this book.

After the building of the daughterboat *Littlesea*, I held a vision for the retired motherboat *Vera*. Finally in 2017, in collaboration with the wheelwrights Mike Rowland & Son, this vision was realised. With support from the Arts Council and a wide range of other funders, *Vera* was given a new lease of life on land. She was upturned and transformed into a miniature maritime museum in which people's memories are preserved and shared. She is called the *Story Boat*. 'Vera the Story Boat' now travels to schools and community events celebrating the story of the lerret. Inside the Story Boat we share the stories of the motherboat and the narratives attached to the 'memory objects' gifted to her. The nets, ropes, floats and stones sing out the stories of the Chesil Bank. It is my hope that in giving a new lease of life to *Vera* and the building of her daughterboat *Littlesea* we are paying homage to the memories of the people who worked the lerrets and their unique contribution to Dorset maritime heritage. I hope their stories will speak for generations to come.

Afterword

There are many more stories and memories swimming along past us; you have to stay on watch. Meanwhile, the history in this book is alive, just out of reach, as the voices linger, reaching us on underwater, sea-bright paths. Reflections of a fish-eye lens. At the heart of this story are mackerel, the local physical environment of Chesil Beach, and a once-fierce dependence of many rural villagers on the sea. Mackerel are no longer our ancient brothers and sisters, our survival; they exist peaceably somewhere nearby for most of us, if we notice them at all.

Memory is social history, individual and collective on the cave walls of our animal skulls. By listening to the stories in this book, giving them space, we tune into local patterns of place identity and personal relationship to individual places, and stories are named and remembered in the dialect of resistance to homogenised language and speech rhythms. By looking back we recall lifestyles, characters and values of a community, and that enables it to continue and maintain a healthy view of itself. Such collective self-awareness of what is important to each community helps perpetuate its very identity. Seine fishing knitted together generations of families, knitted the crews together and bound them to purpose, bound them to the summers and seasons of companionship of mixed generations. There will be no new generation to widely seine and fish as before while there is no hardship or need to return to the perilous shuff of the sea in boats, and younger fishermen would have to relearn how and when to do this, if there were fish.

This is not a polite balance of equilibrium. Small open working boats used to fish on slow seasonal rhythms with everyday awareness of sea-wisdoms and seamanship skills. Mackerel and fishermen in

Opposite: Abbotsbury crew pulling the bundle of fish up the beach. Left to right: Dick Dallet, John Pitman, Unknown, Leonard Christopher, 'Emmet'.

Dorset seaboard villages were bound to their natural environment as hunters and protectors, brief lives to pebbles in the great rumbling roiling lifespan of the great and mighty Chesil. Alan tells me of a particular dolphin pod that the Abbotsbury crew knew by one recognisable dolphin's half dorsal fin, damaged somehow in the War, and every year Ash's crew 'watched the passing of this pod over twenty-seven consecutive summers, though they drove on across the bay in just half an hour. The crew down on the beach all daylight hours of all days of summer bore witness, and they used to always talk about them.'

There is one story told frequently along the Chesil shores. As usual there are no dates to anchor it to any one generation, decade or century. A crew of Portland fishermen were carrying the coffin of their dear captain (we will call him), 'George', back in the day, and en route to the church up the hill, they looked down to the beach and saw the 'wazer's up', mackerel straying… they looked at each other and gently rested the coffin down, saying 'Ol' George would've done the same,' as they hastily rushed back down to the beach and took the shot before resuming their funeral cortège, picking up George from the roadside where they'd left him.

Names carry – same families, same faces, same dorsal fins, same stories cross the same beach, boats and gear gone – but we are as different from our fathers as they were from theirs. Within two generations, much is watered down. We repeat these old stories and we remember together, until repetition and communal memory stirs an alive and dynamic sense of commonality and belonging to place. Celebration of beach. These recordings are living history. While they are read and repeated and trigger more memories shared, they speak to us of our own times.

Appendices

1. Lists of the Park Wall crews
(from Chum Northover's account books 1956–77)

Chummy Northover, Boyce Northover, George Randall (Uncle George), Jack Northover, Stan Northover, Meg Northover, Rod Condliffe, Scott Condliffe, Rex Ireland, Chummy Wiltshire, Charlie Wiltshire, Ron, Stan and Vic Wiltshire. Brian Marshallsay, Toby Marshallsay, David, Edward, Jacob and Bill Mashallsay. Wally Randall, Charlie Randall, Jonny Randall, Shrimpy, Fred, Fred (jr.), Arthur, Chris, Tom, Alfie, Brian, Malcolm and Steven Randall. B. Haynes, G. Farwell, Brian Farwell, Edward Carter, Brian Carter and his son, Steve Stevens, Brian Greensit, Brian Denman, Ray Dalley, David Bartlett, T. (Dutch) Collins, Barry Pearce, B. Lovell, Dolly Grey, Michael Collins, Ken Pearce (Chickerell policeman), J. Guppy, Nick Farn, Brian Farn, Colin Farn, Sugar Farn, Dick Winsor, Charl Legg (snr.), Micky Legg, Charlie Legg, Tomo, Bob (Mink), R. Symes, George Lovell, Len Rolfe, S. Dunford, B Henderson, Bert Rashley (swanherd), Edwin Farn, Bobby 'Duffle' Farn, Rommel Dalley, Johnny Baber, Jim Dalley, Dick Bench, Doug Cross (hairdresser), Derek Andrews, Roger Pearce, Roy Rashley, Richard Legg, A. Buckley, C. Barlow, A. Roberts, G. Kirlew, T. Harris, Ginger, L. Mowlem, Stan Pyne, Brian Honeybun, Tony Beale (policeman after Ken Pearce), Bert Legg, Roy Groves, Malcom Groves, Donald Peach, Walt Handsford, P. Dobson, Les Taylor, R. Scard, Nigel Stevens, Royston Mowlem, Alan Downton, Jim Fall, L. Taylor, M. Waterman, Metcalf, Adrian Weston, Simon Peach, P. David, Martin Hart, M. Pugh, Lyn Davis, Alan Palmer, Derek Moody, Derek Lockhurst, Terry Nethercott, Crusoe, Tug

Wilson, Harold Parker, Bert Cherry, Ian White, John Parker, L. Adams, Gerry Mead, John Masters, George Elliott, Terry Coles, Micky Coles, Gerry Harvey, Roger Honeybun, Doug Lawson, David Greensit, Bert Legg, Bert Merriot, Plummer, E. Stevens, Arthur Knight, Richard Heyler, C. Raisley. A Roberts, Terry Daley, Tom Harries, Chris Barlow, Dave Richards, Gordon Bartlett, Simon Green, Ern, G. Penny, Bert Gibson, M. Baber, Peter Bowring, Tug Richards, Tony Quale, Terry Johnson, Allan Daley, Brian Collins, Adrian Wasson, Graham Wasson.

Boys on a quarter share: Eddie Marshallsay, William, Watts, Ayles, Brian Carter's son, P. Miller, White, K. Bailey, Adams, Scott Condliffe, Tom Kerlew, Nash.

Women on full share: Sybil Legg, Joan Kerlew, Mrs Pearce, Daisy Randall, Mary Oldridge, Mrs Parker.

2. The Fishermen's Instructions and Rules (from Langton Herring)

Of fishing taken from Henry Rose, William Hardy, Thomas Vivian and Ci in the year of our Lord one thousand seven hundred and ninety-two.

Directions – first the owner must find about seine backwater boats, two fish baskets and a bucket for the use of the boat and every article required for the use.

The owner is to chose a man to have a care of the boat and seine to see it properly used and not to geet injured by laying in the boat and to see every man do his best when thaar.

The Captain and the owner must ship twelve men whitch is called seine companey and each man that do agre to the number of twelve to go for the season are so long as convenient according to thear husbandry calling in the werek and every man to the number of twelve must be paid one shelling each by the Captain or the owner which is called the sheninh shilling and not to go with any other company for the season without some just provocasion and then to give the shelling to the owner. And if any man after commencing fishing should be ill and not of his own seeing he is intitled to his shear during the time the Companey is fishing that shipped but not caught they are not to lose thears according to the majority of the Companey wheather it is on cause of drinking or anyother faull of carelessness of thear own. And after that first hundred of mackerall is caught the rulle is for the Companey to go lot by putting each man a peble in a hat that every man must know his own and they must be served out by the Captain that every man may have his day beginning on Munday whitch it is theor duty to acte as buttlers and not to delay in time when sent and not to give away neither in any way to defraud the Companey. And se that the flagin is always cleane and every man according to his day must see the rope bent to the boat after the boat is hulled after shutting. And everyman according to his day is intitled to one mackerall each lot that is caught if over a hundred and when fish is caught it is the Captain's duty to see that men that understand is apointed to count the number and send to seek sutch men that understand selling and when soald give the sample of mackerall called vresk to the buiers as binding the bergin for stch fish being seald. And every reasonable expense is to be paid for thos that go to sell and also those men that take them to whear they are to be carred and when the money is collected to owner and Captain must see the money so earned by the Companey bret forward that every man may asc every expense paid for caring and selling the fish and then the thurd part ois to tacken for the owner and then the oney be aloued to pay for drinck ad the remainder to be devided amoung the number according to whot they have earned of each lot. And any man that first see a lot of fish stray over one reels must avoid smocking or causing any inturuption of aney sort. The Captain may dismis any wen that do not obey the rules and be agreeable with the Caompaney in every with kindness.

3. David Carter's list of lerrets identified from historical documents:

Agnes of Wyke	Faith	Plum
Albert	Fearless	Plum Bunger
Albion	Frolic	Pussy Foot
Aston Villa	General Buller	Queen Mary
Black Beauty	Girl Pat	Rescue
Black Joke	Golden Cap	Rosebud
Blessing	Good Hope	Ruth
Blessing Too	Joan	Sally
Bluebell	Jubilee	Sandy
Britannia	Lark	Sarah
Bug	Linnet	Scarisbrick
Bunger	Luck Liza	Shamrock
Cauliflower	Mackerell	Silver Star
Christina	Mary Anne	Speedwell
Chesil Queen	May	Sunday-At-Home
Comrades	May Queen	Twilight
Dauntless	Navarino	Vera
Dawn	Nellie	Wheatsheaf
Dove	Ping Pong	Why-Not
Ena	Pleasure	Wonder

Further reading

Barnes, W., *The Dorset Poet. A comprehensive Selection of Poetry and Prose*. Dovecote Press, Dorset, 1984.

Evans, G. E., *Where Beards Wag All: The Relevance of Oral Tradition*. Faber, London,1970.

Green, R., *The Making of England*, Macmillan, London, 1882.

Greenhill, B. and Mannering, J., *Inshore Craft: Traditional Working Vessels of the British Isles*. Chatham Publishing, Kent, 1997.

Gutteridge, R., *Dorset Smugglers*. Dorset Publishing Company, 1984.

March, Edgar, J., 2 *Inshore Craft of Britain in the Days of Sail and Oar Volume 2*. David & Charles, London, 1970.

McKee, E., *The Lerrets of Chesil Bank*. The Society of Nautical Research, 1977.

McKee, E., *Working Boats of Britain: Their Shape and Purpose*. Conway Maritime Press, 1988.

Morris, P., *Abbotsbury Historic Landscape Research Project Synthesis Report No. 1.*, Ilchester Estates, 2002.

Seymour, J., *The Companion Guide to The Coast of South-East England*. Harper Collins, London, 1974.

Toms, C., *The Seiners and The Knocker Up. An Autobiographical account of seine fishing on the Chesil Beach*. Cyril Toms, Dorset, 1994.

Acknowledgements

Thanks to Rod and the many people who kindly contributed memories or photos, including: Celia and Tony Harrison; Rex and Jackie Ireland; Pat, Kevin and Perry Donnelly; Winston Maskell; David and Richard Larcombe; Eddie and Paul Stevens; Rab and Sylvia Stone; Nikki Childs; Dennis Harman; Sarah and John West; Pete Pattinson; Steve Matthews; David Carter; Gary Downton; Richard Samways; Alan Arnold; Pete Stevens; Mike Smyth; Pete and Pearl Parsons; Phil and Pat Hutchings; Nancy, Tracey and Ricky Gape, Mike Beale, Sandra Fretwell, Eddie Marshallsay and Ian Reeder. Thanks to the generous time, passion and expertise of contributors Pat Corbett, Don Moxom, Anne Brown, Gail McGarva and to photographers Keith Pritchard, George Wright and Pauline Rook.

Thanks for information and research to the team at the Dorset History Centre; The West Bay Discovery Centre; Liam Coles at The Lugger Inn, Chickerell; Shire Hall Historic Courthouse Museum; Portland Museum Collection; Weymouth Museum Collection and Dorset Library services. Thanks to Gail McGava for her 2011 recordings. Thanks to Naomi Cudmore for friendship and sea journeys, and to Dan Bryant for everything. Thanks to Little Toller for their patience, care and craft. And thanks to Chesil Beach, a place I love and dream.